T0144670

A ROAD MAP FOR
Life's Detours

A ROAD MAP FOR
Life's Detours

FINANCIAL GUIDANCE AND MORE FOR EVERY WOMAN

PLANNING
FOR THE
Unexpected

CAROL M. KHOURI

CFP®, CDFA™, CeFT®

Advantage®

Published by Advantage, Charleston, South Carolina.
Member of Advantage Media Group.

ADVANTAGE is a registered trademark, and the Advantage colophon is a trademark of Advantage Media Group, Inc.

Printed in the United States of America.

10 9 8 7 6 5 4 3 2 1

ISBN: 978-1-59932-547-7
LCCN: 2017942405

Cover design by George Stevens.
Layout design by Megan Elger.

This publication is designed to provide accurate and authoritative information in regard to the subject matter covered. It is sold with the understanding that the publisher is not engaged in rendering legal, accounting, or other professional services. If legal advice or other expert assistance is required, the services of a competent professional person should be sought.

Advantage Media Group is proud to be a part of the Tree Neutral® program. Tree Neutral offsets the number of trees consumed in the production and printing of this book by taking proactive steps such as planting trees in direct proportion to the number of trees used to print books. To learn more about Tree Neutral, please visit www.treeneutral.com.

Advantage Media Group is a publisher of business, self-improvement, and professional development books and online learning. We help entrepreneurs, business leaders, and professionals share their Stories, Passion, and Knowledge to help others Learn & Grow. Do you have a manuscript or book idea that you would like us to consider for publishing? Please visit **advantagefamily.com** or call **1.866.775.1696**.

Table of Contents

About the Author

CAROL KHOURI is an accomplished financial advisor who specializes in creating financial solutions for women. With more than twenty-five years of experience, her approach involves comprehensive financial planning, unbiased investment management, and establishing partnerships with other specialists as needed to ensure a cohesive, long-term plan.

Change can be unsettling. For women facing life-altering events, change can also be financially devastating. Many women find themselves unprepared for the financial challenges that change often creates. Carol is an expert at helping women identify and avoid potential monetary hazards. By creating personalized financial planning strategies, she can help her clients become more financially sound and secure.

After working closely with her clients to develop a customized strategy to reach their goals, Carol remains actively involved in the process to ensure that her clients have consistent support for their everyday needs. She has helped hundreds of women overcome the often complex financial challenges posed by life-changing events such as divorce, retirement, elder care, and the loss of a spouse. By providing ongoing education and guidance, Carol's ultimate objective is to empower women during their transitions and beyond.

Carol prides herself on being able to help her clients navigate their financial affairs during the most stressful times of their lives. In addition to being a Certified Financial Planner®, a Certified Divorce Financial Analyst™, and Certified Financial Transitionist®, she has been honored by her colleagues and clients with Five-Star Wealth Manager recognition.

Introduction

I never intended to be a financial advisor; I started in the business back in 1986, when it was predominantly a man's field. I fell into it by chance; I applied to a job posting in Boston. At that time, I had a good friend working downtown and thought we could commute together. I was initially hired for a job opening in operations but subsequently moved to another firm, where I was introduced to client services and then promoted to an advisory position. I felt empowered, not because I had moved up the job ladder, but because I discovered how much I enjoyed helping people.

I have a passion for educating people about money, investments, and retirement planning. It is essential to me that my clients understand why balance matters in their investment allocation. I want to make them active partners in creating their financial plans, so they learn to recognize all the moving parts of their economic well-being. It is important for them to become familiar with concepts like risk tolerance, future and present value, dollar-cost averaging, and much more. With an improved working knowledge of finances, my clients have a better grasp of how their money is invested to meet their needs and objectives, balanced with their tolerance for risk.

Unfortunately, a fair number of women in my generation, as well as those that came before me, are ill-informed about money. Their lack of financial understanding can and does lead to unfortunate and sometimes devastating outcomes, particularly if these women's lives change in some way that suddenly leaves them with the sole responsibility for managing their assets. I give my clients a better sense of why they own certain assets, why they need to remain invested, and how this impacts their end goals.

In the 1980s, the business of finance was mostly transactional; brokers made cold calls chiefly with the intent of making money, selling products to people because it was all commission based. There was virtually no concept of basic financial planning for most people. Fortunately, this climate has changed and continues to improve as people realize that financial knowledge and proper planning provides a sound road map for their future.

While I recognized the shortfalls women could face in the financial world, I did not truly understand the unique challenges women faced until my own divorce. I, someone with a background and knowledge of finances, was distraught and overwhelmed, having to rebalance my life around a smaller income and more significant expenses. If I could barely get through—running spreadsheets, creating budgets, stressing over making ends meet—I was left wondering how someone without my financial expertise could even begin to cope. That's when it hit me: I needed to be a specialist. How could I help other women who were facing these kinds of obstacles in their lives?

I have some very sophisticated clients who have been managing their finances for years, but I also have other clients who have never written a check, much less paid a bill on their own. So, my women clients run the gamut regarding their financial expertise and understanding, but in my view, there is a common thread: they have different needs and a different relationship with money than men.

For women, it's about security and understanding what they need to do to reach their end goals. It is a matter of knowing that they are investing in a way that will provide them with a dependable income stream and, hopefully, a legacy that can be transferred to their children, or other loved ones.

There are plenty of sudden and unwelcome life changes that can cast your finances into question, such as widowhood, illness, or even a job loss. Like many women, I have experienced firsthand the trauma of losing a job; I felt as though I had lost my identity. In a way, it was worse than my divorce, and it came just as my divorce was wrapping up. I thought about the women who did not work, women who had been "Mrs. Somebody" most of their adult lives and who did not have the advantage of a career outside the home and an income of their own. They were losing their identities, too. The loss of an income stream leaves women with questions such as *"Where am I going to end up? How am I going to survive through all of this?"* For women who were financially well-off, their day-to-day lives would at least be secure, but for the majority of middle-class women, that is not the case; they may have to make significant changes in their lifestyles to accommodate their new circumstances. They need to focus on planning for their futures; they need help creating a road map for life's detours. This book is designed to help you prepare for the unexpected. I develop financial plans for my clients to help them get where they want to go. Events happen in life; some of them you can potentially predict and plan for, but others, like the sudden death of a spouse, come out of nowhere. More and more, I've been hearing clients say, *"My friend's husband just died unexpectedly, and he did not have any life insurance."*

Knowledge plus planning is power. We can't control every part of life, but getting a handle what we can control, provides peace of mind. For example, having a plan can minimize the stress in figuring out what you and your late spouse have in retirement funds, insurance policies, or other investments. Grieving the loss of a spouse is hard—and grieving with the added worries and burdens of not knowing how you'll meet your financial obligations in the future is exponentially worse.

Recently, I received a call from a woman overcome with grief due to the loss of her husband; she did not know anything about financial matters. She had no clue where to start or what to do. All she could manage was to pile her mail, her husband's documents and anything that looked important into boxes and bring them to my office. We went through it all, and that was the basis of her financial plan. It was a tough one because her circumstances had changed radically, and she had to make some difficult decisions very quickly while under a vast amount of stress.

Situations similar to the one just described can be minimized or even avoided. This book is designed to help you know more about your finances, more about your options, and more about planning. We will walk through some of the possible scenarios, and we will suggest ways to avoid the worst circumstances.

My goal is to present you with the facts as clearly and logically as possible, and I promise, by the time you get to the last page of this book, you'll put it down feeling safer and more financially savvy and confident then you do now.

Chapter One

CHARTING THE COURSE

As a financial planner and advisor, I've seen it too many times: women hit a turn in their lives and are left, for whatever reason, without the income they have come to expect. Suddenly, they are on their own without any real knowledge of their resources or how they are invested; some women do not even know what being "invested" means. I have worked with women who do not have a clue about their expenses or their finances. Even if you think your life is financially secure, don't take it for granted or assume that this will always be the case. Knowledge is power, and there is no better time than right now to start pulling together the information you need to secure your future.

By the time a client comes to me for the first time, she has often already made mistakes that will cost her time and money. In cases of divorce, for instance, I find that women schedule an appointment with me after the divorce is finalized, rather than during the process. One distraught woman called me saying she felt poorly represented with other specialists she hired for her divorce. She told me she wanted my advice. I asked, *"Is the divorce finalized?"* She replied that she could still make changes; so, I said, "*Okay, send me the draft of the proposal.*" When I received the document, I realized it was the final decree, and everything was already signed and sealed. I was unable to assist with her divorce because it was finalized. I explained to her that the document had been approved and settled by the court and legal system. It was signed by the judge, her ex-husband and herself. It was as good as etched in stone. In a divorce, once the agreement is approved and finalized, you can never go back and change the division of assets. The only two provisions you can modify after a divorce is complete are the child support and alimony payments.

This client would have benefitted from a better understanding of the documents put before her. A good rule of thumb is to be completely clear on what you're signing before you sign it. Ask for help if there is something you do not understand. Get the clarification you need and deserve. In my experience, women are more likely to sign away their possessions than men; women just want the situation resolved and all the legal wrangling to stop, so they typically sign what is put in front of them.

I met with two women whose spouses passed away without having made any comprehensive plans for their future support. Had there been some planning before they were widowed, we could have identified a need for life insurance for the first woman, and we would have recommended estate planning for a more secure future for the second woman.

Women in situations like these need to take advantage of financial planners who have experience with proprietary planning software that can forecast twenty or thirty years down the road. When I start working on a financial plan, I consider income streams, expenses, goals, and risk tolerance to predict what my client will need today, tomorrow and well into the future. I provide valuable information about allocating assets effectively to meet future needs.

In my many years of experience, I can't help wonder how so many smart women fall into the trap of financial illiteracy. Part of the problem is that many of us are okay with leaving the financial planning piece of our lives to our husbands. We may be so busy with our careers and raising our children that we do not have time to even think about finances. We may make routine financial decisions for the household, but are we looking at the big picture? Sometimes, that's how our husbands like it: they do not want to deal with the day-to-day finances but prefer to control the major planning. This is likely how your parents' finances worked, so it is familiar and comfortable. But it shouldn't be. There are basic financial facts you must know, and it is fair game to ask your spouse about household finances and to get involved in big financial decisions. Your loved one should want you to know about these matters, especially when he understands that not knowing could negatively impact your future.

KEEP YOUR RECORDS TOGETHER

The first order of business you need to address is identifying where your financial records are kept. Evaluate what you own in terms of investments, insurance policies, savings, and debts. It is essential to be organized and to be ahead of need, so please don't wait; start today. I have a very small household; it's just my son and me. I created a folder in my file cabinet at home that's labeled, "Just In Case." In that file, my son can see every life insurance policy, every investment, and any other assets I own. I have documented contact information for every holding, including phone numbers, addresses, websites, emails, etc. I've also told my son that if he can't handle it when I'm gone, he can take the whole folder to my office, and the people there will help him. Note: It is crucial to update the folder as the information changes. A stagnant folder can be more confusing than not having one at all.

Do you have an emergency financial file in your home, one that's up-to-date and that you're already familiar with? If you don't, you need to create one. And it's not hard to do, even if you're the type who has not paid much attention to your finances. Take time to have a conversation with your spouse. Say, "*Honey, you know what? I was reading this book, and it makes a lot of sense. If you pass away before me, I am going to be so distraught and upset, and I'm going to need help. Is there a way we can build a file that contains all the information I need to know in the event you die first?*"

I know it's a hard topic to discuss, but it will save you hours of frustration, and possibly money, if you do it now, before you need the information.

WHAT SHOULD MY EMERGENCY FINANCIAL INFORMATION FILE CONTAIN?

Here's a list of the documents and information your file should contain:

- ☐ Investment accounts
- ☐ 529 accounts
- ☐ Bank accounts
- ☐ Retirement accounts
- ☐ Beneficiary designations (on all financial accounts and life insurance policies)

- ☐ Insurance information (home, auto, life, long-term care, disability)
- ☐ Wills, trusts, health care proxies (know the location of originals)
- ☐ Living will or advanced directive (end-of-life choices)
- ☐ Power-of-attorney forms
- ☐ Credit card information
- ☐ Credit rating information
- ☐ Mortgage documents
- ☐ Deed to the home (if paid off)
- ☐ Automobile title (if paid off)
- ☐ Preplanned funeral arrangements (if any)
- ☐ Health coverage documentation
- ☐ Military records (many towns have tax abatements for military personnel and spouses)
- ☐ Employer-survivorship benefits (if any)
- ☐ Loan paperwork (auto, education, home-equity loan)

QUESTIONS YOU NEED ANSWERED:

Where is our money? How is it invested? Where is it held?

Are your household finances invested through a broker, or are they held with a registered investment advisor? Is there someone helping you manage your investments? If so, who is that person, and what is his or her contact information?

What type of insurance policies do you have and on whom?

If you have life insurance policies, identify the company that holds them. Find out how much they are worth, and know who is listed as the beneficiaries. Most life insurance information is located on the annual statement. Determine if you have mortgage insurance, and if so, for how much?

What do you know about your home?

If you have a mortgage, know which company holds it. Get a copy of your mortgage statement to know the contract terms such as your interest rate and the length of your loan. If you have a balloon payment, you may want to consider refinancing when interest rates are low. Do you have equity in your home? To calculate your home equity, take the current value of your home minus your outstanding liens on your property. If you are planning on selling your home, you need to determine your cost basis. Your cost basis should reflect what you paid for your home plus any renovations or upgrades and the cost to sell it. Note, your cost basis can also be reduced if you receive rental income on your home, if you deducted part of your home as a business, or if you receive a windfall such as an eminent domain payment.

What is my credit rating?

It's important to know your credit rating. At some point, you may have to refinance your home, buy a car, or another big-ticket item. The company you are buying from or refinancing through is going to look at your credit rating. To check your credit score go to www. consumer.ftc.gov. If it is below seven hundred, you may not fare too well. If you have been a housewife or stay-at-home mom your whole life and if the credit cards have been under your husband's name, then you may not have a favorable credit score. But you can take steps to head that off now. Open your own credit card account and establish a line of credit. Start the process by visiting your local bank. Talk with a bank representative about applying for a credit card. Pay off the amount due every month. Make sure payments are on time and never late. If you have adult children, this is something they too should be doing. Encourage them to start their financial record in their junior year of college, especially if you do not want to be co-signing loans.

How much debt do you have?

Whether you're talking about death or divorce, debt is very important. Ask yourself; is the debt so large that you can't finance it? Your debt level may be fine as long as the income level is there to support it, but if there is a sudden loss of income, the debt level can quickly become too high, and you may no longer be able to meet the monthly payments. You don't want to have to file for bankruptcy protection; it's traumatizing, both personally and financially. If you have a significant amount of debt, it might be wise to start paying it down ahead of time. Alternately, you could consider getting life insurance for the main breadwinner, in the event of death, the debts can be paid off.

How much is being contributed to a retirement savings plan, and where is it?

Your spouse can have one or more individual retirement accounts (IRAs) and/or a company 401(k) plan. If your spouse is self-employed, he/she may have a SEP or a Simple IRA or an individual 401(k). I have spoken with people who changed their jobs and left their money in their 401(k) plan. Although they had not worked for the firm for years, their money is still in their account, and they have forgotten about it. If something were to happen to you and you had funds in a 401(k), be aware that the administrator of the 401(k) plan isn't going to be looking for you, so you need to know what you have and where it is. Also, be aware of the plan's regulations because the rules at each company can be slightly different. One company may allow you to retain the assets in the plan; another may force a distribution.

Do you have 529 or other custodial accounts for the children or grandchildren?

College saving plans such as 529 accounts can be opened by parents, grandparents, or anyone wishing to contribute toward a child's college savings. If you are aware of someone setting up an account for your child, you need to know how much the account is worth, how the funds are invested, and you should obtain the contact information for the plan administrator.

Know who the beneficiaries are on your accounts.

Not only should your beneficiaries be designated on all your financial accounts and policies, but they should be updated as well. Forgetting to change recipients can lead to problems. More often than not, people in second marriages forget to change heirs on their accounts or insurance policies when they remarry. Furthermore, in a divorce, there may be a requirement to hold a life insurance policy for the ex-spouse if children are involved. Not knowing this crucial information is the kind of surprise you want to avoid, so make sure you understand what benefits go where.

Is there an up-to-date will/health care proxy/power of attorney?

A will, health care proxy and power of attorney are vital documents that protect you in case of an emergency. If you have not completed any of these legal documents or if they are outdated, it is time to get these vital papers in order. Remember, these are legal documents you should have duly signed and notarized and then have copies of them in your emergency folder. If your will is held with your attorney, make sure you have contact information for the lawyer. If you have adult children in college, you may want to have a health care proxy in place for them, so you can be informed of their health condition if something were to happen to them while away at college. It is essential to know where original documents are kept. If you are in need of creating these documents, contact an attorney.

Do you have an advance directive?

The purpose of an advance directive is to allow you to express your desires regarding your medical treatment should you be in a situation where you are unable to communicate your preferences. This document includes such items as "do not resuscitate" orders and instructions regarding other types of life-sustaining treatment. It is important to note this health care form is directed by each state and can have different names accordingly. Your attorney can prepare the advance directive document, or you can obtain the form from your health care provider or local health care facility and complete it yourself.

Where does the money go? What bills are paid and how?

Very often in a marriage, one spouse handles the bill paying, and it amazes me how often the other spouse has no clue about the expenses or how they are paid. If your husband has auto-pay on accounts and you don't know that, you could wind up paying your bills twice if something were to happen to him. If banking and bill paying are set up online, you need an up-to-date record of login IDs and passwords so that you can access the online accounts. Remember to revisit and update this information regularly.

What is your monthly cash flow?

Monthly cash flow is your net income minus your average monthly expenses. Are you making more than you're spending, breaking even, or chipping away at your savings? If you are bringing in $12,000 a month and paying out $7,000, you have a $5,000 surplus each month. If you're spending $15,000 a month and you're only bringing in $12,000, then you have a $3,000 deficit every month, and that's growing, since that $3,000 deficit is probably being financed through credit cards, with compound interest causing it to get larger every month. I advise my clients to start with an Excel file and input all income in one column and outflows in a second column. If you have no idea of your spending or income, review your bank and credit card statements. Analyze the last twelve months of reports to determine your cash flow.

Where are your tax returns for the last seven years?

In the event you face a tax audit, did you know you will need to have copies of your records for seven years past your last filing? I find it best to keep an expandable file folder for each year with all documents pertaining to that tax year in a file cabinet. If you prefer to keep a digital record, remember to store it on a secure site or disc.

Did your spouse serve in the military?

If you or your spouse served in the military, keep those records accessible, because you may be eligible for additional benefits from Veterans Affairs. Also, many cities and towns have some form of tax credit for service personnel.

Do you need a parental nomination of guardian?

If you are the parent(s) of underage children, the parental nomination of guardian is very important. Have you ever considered what would happen to your children if you and your husband go out one night and do not make it home? In most situations, regulations require the police to place your children in the care of the Department of Children and Families (DCF). If you have a will that designates the custodial arrangements of your children in the event of your death, your children can be held at DCF until your attorney can submit the proper paperwork to have them released into the loving hands of the person(s) you elected to care for them. Do you believe placing your child with DCF is the best short-term solution? No, is the simple answer here, and DCF placement is easily avoided. The parental nomination of a guardian is a legal document (prepared by an attorney). Once established, you can make copies available to the babysitter, your parents, and any other appropriate party. This document will dictate where your children should be placed immediately after a crisis situation.

In summary, if you have the answers to these questions in writing in a file that is safely stored, then you are in good shape—congratulations! Make sure that you and your spouse are not the only ones who know about this file, consider sharing it with an adult child, trustworthy family member, friend or perhaps your attorney - it can save the people you leave behind a lot of time and grief.

I occasionally run seminars on financial literacy for my female clients. A couple of months ago, a woman who planned to attend my seminar called saying, *"I'm so sorry, I can't make it to your seminar. You know, one of these days I have to sit down with you because I know nothing about these matters."* A month later, she called to tell me that her husband had suddenly passed away. She was distraught and completely lost. She had no clue how things were going to play out; she never took an active role in being prepared. She was left not knowing anything about her financial situation. Since her initial phone call, we have met numerous times, and I developed and prioritized a task list. I built her a budget and created a financial plan. She was basically starting at zero. She needed to spend a fair amount of time and money to get her life in order.

I tell my clients that there are a lot of things we can't control in life, but there are also things we can control, and those things need to be managed to protect ourselves as well as those we love. Life can deal some hard, quick blows. Being prepared and knowledgeable can mitigate at least some of the pain and confusion that these trying times leave in their wake.

Action Checklist

Chapter One: Charting the Course

- ☐ Create a "Just In Case" file.

- ☐ Check your credit score.

- ☐ Complete a parental nomination of guardian for minor children.

- ☐ Draw up a will, health care proxy, and power of attorney.

- ☐ Discuss and write up advance directives.

- ☐ Have adult children in college or at home, complete a health care proxy that identifies you as an "agent" who can be informed about their medical condition and make health care decisions if they are unable to communicate those decisions themselves.

- ☐ Establish a budget: What money is coming in, what money is flowing out, and how is it being spent?

- ☐ Make a balance sheet of what you own and what you owe.

Chapter Two

YOUR FINANCIAL CHECKUP

One of the key benefits of putting together your "Just In Case" file is having a general working knowledge of your financial picture. You should know how much money you have coming in, and how much money you have going out every month. You should know if you are saving on a regular basis, just breaking even, or going into debt, and who holds that debt. Now that you have a picture of your cash flow, it is time to start thinking about putting these numbers together and making a plan. Ask yourself, *"Do I have enough savings? How much more do I need to save to secure my future, to reach my goals and objectives?"*

If the term "financial plan" sounds intimidating, think of it as a road map that leads you to an understanding of whether you have enough money saved for your current lifestyle if something were to change. If you realize there isn't enough for your future, you can figure out how to accumulate the necessary funds. This is important no matter how much money you make or what tax bracket you are in, and there is a solution for every set of circumstances.

If you and your husband have a budget of $12,000 per month, and have saved $1.2 million, chances are you are not going to be able to make ends meet after some years because your expenses are far more than what that $1.2 million is going to generate for your income needs. Instead of entering retirement saying, "*I think I have plenty of money to meet my needs*" you are wise to ask "*Do I have enough savings? Do I need more funds to meet my financial goals?*" Having a financial plan will answer that question for you. Ask yourself, "*Do I have enough money to retire?*" and "*If I need to accumulate more money, what do I have to do? Where do I cut? What do I have to reevaluate? Can I lower my expenses? Where is the money going to come from for me to be able to save more?*" A sound financial plan eliminates a lot of these questions and provides a realistic framework, rather than a series of "what ifs."

DISCRETIONARY SPENDING VERSUS NECESSITIES

One of the first discussions I have when working with a client trying to increase their asset base is about the distinction between discretionary spending and necessary spending. Discretionary spending is the money you use to buy non-essential items. Vacation is typically thought to be a discretionary expense, as is money spent on hobbies. When you think of your discretionary budget, consider these questions: Are you shopping at high-end retail stores or mid-range stores? Do you look for sales and clearance items? Do you use coupons? A little creative buying can do wonders for your wardrobe. Consider buying a few coordinated pieces and mix them up to turn five separate outfits into ten. There are always ways around having to up-end your whole lifestyle, and sometimes a piece of that is as simple as changing the way you shop.

When you begin to set up a budget, think to yourself: *If I am spending $12,000 and I can only afford $7,000, how do I bring the $12,000 down to $7,000?* Obviously, there are fixed costs that you cannot change: your mortgage is a set amount that you are going to have to pay. You may, however, be able to lower your electric bill more than you think. Instead of leaving all the lights on, shut them off and conserve. When you replace an appliance, consider purchasing energy-efficient products. What about your weekly food budget? Where are you shopping? Do you frequent high-end grocery stores or establishments where you can get better value? Do you purchase more food than you need? These are the things you must consider to meet the goal of decreasing your spending. Sometimes it may be the realization that you cannot keep that luxury car because the maintenance is cost prohibitive, and you can replace a luxury vehicle with one that's going to cost less to keep on the road. It comes down to what is more important to you: Do you value living for today or having enough for tomorrow? Some people want to live just for today, and in such cases, these people are going to be working their whole lives, and their hopes for a comfortable retirement are slim. They will have to accept responsibility for the path they chose to take. When they are sixty-five or seventy years old and want to retire, that may not be possible because of the choices they made when they were forty or fifty years old. An unwillingness to forfeit luxury items and an expensive lifestyle has consequences.

SOONER IS BETTER

Many of my married clients make a decent salary. One couple, in particular, came to me last year asking for advice. They have young children, a big house, fancy cars—seemingly everything. He had a lot of debt due to medical school loans, and she was worried about their future. We had a frank discussion. We looked at the numbers, talked about options, and they chose to sell the big house and luxury cars. That allowed them to pay off their loans. They are renting a house right now. They will buy a home when they can afford it, and in the meantime, they are putting away $6,000 per month. By downsizing ahead of any pressing need to do so, they are creating a healthy cash flow in the right direction and will not be stuck for years servicing that debt. The choice was easy when they considered the option of having increased debt years down the road and not enough savings for retirement.

Did you know, according to the Social Security Administration, a woman turning age sixty-five today can expect to live, on average, an additional 21.6 years? In addition, one out of every four people will live past age ninety, and one out of ten will live past age ninety-five.[1] That means we need to think ahead and look for ways to save more money now and then find ways to make our money last.

Of course, I hear from some clients: *"I'm going to be so senile by then it won't even matter, so why save? I'll be on Medicaid or in a nursing home, and I will not be cognizant of where I am."* My response is simple, *"Maybe or maybe not. Are you willing to bet your life on it?"* I recently spoke with a gentleman who said, *"I was out playing tennis today, and the best player on the court was a ninety-one-year-old."* And this gentleman is eighty-three! He is living in a continuing-care facility surrounded by other healthy, active folks in their eighties and nineties. He realized it's a good thing he planned ahead. He frequently remarks, *"Hey, I could live another ten years because there is physically nothing wrong with me."*

1   "Social Security Is Important to Women," Social Security Administration, June 2015, https://www.ssa.gov/news/press/factsheets/women.htm.

As women get older, they should ask themselves, "*Can I continue to afford this lifestyle, even if my spouse dies? Am I going to have enough money to survive his loss?*" Unfortunately, many of us do not consider these questions until it is too late. Most people put off retirement planning until just before they are about to retire. Retirement planning is about saving today for the future. Retirement planning is done when you are still employed and have the means to save money.

The sooner you start evaluating your situation and begin saving, the better. The husband and wife I described earlier, with the high loan burden, are only in their forties, but they are looking ahead, and they will be glad they did. They are addressing their debts while they are working, while there is income, and while there is a way to save. They will not wrongly assume that because they worked their whole lives, spent their money discerningly, and have a $2 million 401(k) plan, that they have enough to retire. Far too often I have worked with couples who believed they were all set for retirement because they had one to two million dollars in their saving accounts. However, they took no responsibility for evaluating their spending. Such situations typically do not bode well, especially when expenses are high.

It is necessary to have a good handle on all your financial information, to have it all in one location, to know how you stack up, and to use that information as a starting point for a financial plan. Take that material to a financial planner and share it. Once you know where you are today, you will have an idea where you will be twenty or thirty years from now. Of course, it will be a projection— but the projections are fact-based and can be instrumental in helping you plan for your future. Yes, there will be bumps in the road. Yes, there will be detours, but if you're continually updating and reviewing your financial plan every year, you will be prepared.

WHAT GOES INTO YOUR FINANCIAL PLAN?

By creating a financial plan, you are building a financial road map. The more accurate your input data, the more precise will be your plan. Financial planning allows you to have some indication of how your current expenditures will affect your retirement. The report will provide you with statistical data to help determine how much savings you need to support your current lifestyle in retirement and where that money is going to come from. Part of your income will come from Social Security, and a portion will be from your 401(k) plan and savings account(s); if you're lucky enough to work for a corporation that has a pension plan, then that will provide additional monies. We start a financial plan by pulling all these pieces together to get an understanding of your future cash flow. This doesn't just apply to people who have a million or more dollars. This kind of thinking is useful for everyone.

If you are carrying student debt, then you are likely losing money servicing your loans. While you may be earning a decent salary, you need to evaluate the loan payments you are making with respect to your salary. If you are spending a good portion of your income to pay down your debts and obligations with virtually nothing left to put aside in savings, your lifestyle may be unsustainable. I'm not saying you must alter your entire spending habits, but I am saying that you need to be aware of the choices you are making and their consequences.

One of my clients, a physician, and his wife raised four children. The physician is ready to retire today. Despite having created a plan years ago, he recently realized that he couldn't retire—although he had saved a substantial amount of money, he and his wife could not live on the income his savings would generate. Why? They live too extravagantly: (1) they frequently give money to their children; (2)

they shop exclusively at specialty food stores and high-end retail shops; and (3) they are not willing to give up any of it. When I showed them their financial picture, they were stunned; we talked, and I explained that they needed to cut their monthly budget by $5,000 and put that money away. They were determined. We got it done. Together we developed a plan for reducing those unnecessary expenses to save money. Honestly, I'm pretty sure they were not clear on just how much they spent up to that point—they never had a dose of reality quite like that before. If you have grown up with the freedom to buy, it is easy habit to continue spending and to support your children unnecessarily. I reminded this couple that their children were in their thirties, and it was time for them to look after themselves.

I was recently at a fundraiser and happened to sit next to a professional athlete who told me he makes nearly $8 million a year. When we started talking about his financial future, I quickly realized he was spending close to what he made. I couldn't help but ask, *"How can you possibly spend millions of dollars per year?"* *"It is easy,"* he said. *"There are years I am strapped for funds because it is so easy to spend."* The lesson here is that money must be managed, no matter how much one makes.

Spending on children and grandchildren can bring so much joy, but it can bring hardship as well. It is easy to give more than you can truly afford. I have a divorced client in her early sixties living in Arizona with an investment account totaling just under a quarter of a million dollars. Her daughter lives in Chicago. She recently divorced. My client continuously gives her daughter money to make ends meet. On average, she gives $1,000 to her daughter each month. I understand her passion for helping her child, but if she continues spending like this, in four short years, she will go through all her money without even thinking about it. My client is short-sighted and living for today. In stark contrast, I have a client in her eighties who put away close to one million dollars on a modest salary. She frequently worried about spending too much money and tightened her budget in her early fifties to have enough funds to last the rest of her life. I recommend a good, quick rule of thumb to follow: You can withdraw roughly 4 percent of your saved assets on an annualized basis once you are retired. By sticking with a 4 percent withdrawal rate, your money will most likely outlive you, and you will potentially have funds remaining for your legacy.

For example, let's consider a newly retired couple with $1 million in a 401(k) plan. The couple can realistically withdraw $40,000 a year, which is going to give them about $3,000 per month in retirement. Then we add in Social Security; let's assume that together, they will receive $3,000 to $4,000 each month. This couple will have roughly a budget of $6,000–$7,000 per month. Now let's consider a single person with the same level of retirement savings; her/his Social Security would likely be about $1,900 to $2,200 per month. That person is looking at a total of $4,000 to $5,000 a month in income.

In these examples, the monthly estimates are what people have as a maximum budget. If they have been spending more than that, then they must curtail their spending. It is that simple. Note, in these examples, the retiree does not have any debt to pay. Therefore, the earnings typically result in $150 of income a day if single or $215 if married. But what happens when there are other expenses? What happens if a couple has a high mortgage and is trying to pay it down while managing high medical payments and credit card debt? These issues are critical. You must be aware of all your expenses, and plan for them. Theoretically, it is nice to set things up so that the day you decide to retire; you are also able to pay off your mortgage. Not servicing that debt is a relief and provides extra cash flow.

I recently had lunch with a client; she's married and has a couple of children. Her husband makes plenty of money, and they have nothing to worry about. However, she is concerned that her son may not be able to afford college for her granddaughter, so she asked: "*Can I open up a 529 plan? I want to put money aside so that I can help my granddaughter with college expenses.*" I replied, "*We need to come up with a plan. We need to put all your wishes, goals, and objectives down on paper and then look at your spending and income. Let's look at your assets, put everything together, and see how much you can afford.*" It is important to go through this process before you say, "Y*es, do it.*" My client has many generous goals—she wants to bequeath a portion of her mother's estate to her children and to help them out in various ways—but first, she must understand how much she can afford to give away. Taking time to do this is going to give her the answers she needs. If she does not do the planning, she can quickly end up giving a significant amount of her money away and then find herself struggling in her late eighties. Given that her mother is a healthy ninety-three-year-old today, the chances are good that my client will live well into her nineties.

I do understand that these thoughts are upsetting, and you may be thinking, *If I am unable to give to my grandchildren and if I cannot buy items I want, then what is this all about?* I'm not saying you can't do either of these things; rather, you must simply be aware of how much extra money you have. If you do a budget and you have a surplus, and you have enough money being put aside for your retirement—then yes, enjoy spending those extra dollars. Go out, spend it, buy things for your children and grandchildren. If you do your budget and you're running in the red, and there is no surplus, however, then you simply are not saving enough in your retirement accounts for your future. You will be fooling yourself if you do not take corrective action soon. Eventually, reality will catch up with you. In the long run; it's far better to buckle down and save now so that you can be self-reliant, not just for your sake but for the sake of your children as well.

After my divorce, over sixteen years ago, I had to change my lifestyle. The big, new house was gone, and I scaled down to a much smaller, older home. Would I have liked to redo my kitchen? Yes, and I would have loved to remodel my bathroom too—but I settled for doing the smaller, less-expensive fixes, like painting and putting in new floors. Yes, when the holidays came, I missed my double oven, my pantry, my island—a lot of things. All those amenities were cut out of my life because I needed to downsize. I needed to be able to save more money. It was a reality check. I had to come to grips with the understanding that I was not going to get alimony, and that child support wasn't going to be of substance because my ex wasn't working. As time went by, I made some home improvements because I was able to budget for them. Today, my kitchen and bathrooms have been renovated. I still watch my money. I don't buy new cars; I buy used cars around five years old with low mileage. Yes, I have to make the time to find the best deal, but those deals are out there. I snagged a gorgeous Mercedes S Class at an estate sale for probably two-thirds of what I would have had to pay a dealer, so I have my luxury car and my money too! It's a safe car, which matters most to me because I drive a lot. I want to remind my clients that they can still have some or all of the things that they want; they just have to be sure that their decisions are SMART (Specific, Measurable, Attainable, Relevant, and Timely) from a financial perspective.

WHERE DOES THE MONEY GO?

It's not hard to begin to keep tabs on your spending—it takes some effort to start, but once you establish a routine, it is easy to manage. Start by reviewing your credit card statements. Many online credit card apps allow you to sort your transactions by date, retailer, category, amount, etc. These data sorts can be saved as Excel worksheets on your computer where you can keep a running account of your spending. I recommend that you review your credit card spending every month. See where and what consumes most of your dollars. Think about where you could make cuts in the future. You will also want to review your checking account. Bank statements help you see what you are paying out monthly. Review your canceled checks and your statements to see automated electronic payments that occur regularly. Utilize whatever means is easiest and readily available. I advise my clients who aren't inclined to keep good records to use our online secure money management system, which gives them the ability to aggregate all their spending from multiple banks, and credit card companies. Some of my savvy accounting clients subscribe to QuickBooks; a bookkeeping software program that facilitates proper record keeping. It makes the budgeting procedure simple and clear, which helps start the process.

Other spending considerations include a review of the number of times you ask for cash back when you write a check or use a debit card at the market. You should also consider how quickly you are at the ATM withdrawing money.

With the relatively untraceable nature of cash, holding yourself accountable for how and where you spend money is more difficult to track than other forms of payment. Are you at a coffee shop every morning? Are you buying lunch regularly or ordering pizza for dinner? Are you giving your kids money? Maybe you need to reconsider all those things to reduce your spending. One of my clients, a couple with young children, needed to start saving $5,000 per month for their children's college savings accounts. I reviewed their cash spending and saw that they ate out nearly every night. That was a significant financial drain. I asked them what they got for it, and they replied, "large waistlines!" It takes a mindset to break habits, but it can be done, and once successful, the reward is well worth it. That same couple now has over $150,000 in their children's 529 college fund accounts, and their children are under the age of fifteen.

When preparing for retirement, it makes sense to look at the investment you have made in your home. If you have built up a sizable amount of equity and live in a desirable area, you may want to think about downsizing once the children are out of the house. While investing in a home may have been profitable, it is illiquid and unable to help provide monthly income. Being able to downsize releases the equity you have built and allows you to invest in more liquid assets that can help ensure monthly cash flow in retirement. In addition, if done right, you should be able to decrease your monthly expenses.

It is not uncommon for homeowners to decide to sell the expensive home with the goal to save on mortgage payments and taxes and to put away for retirement. Moreover, some homeowners decide to move to states such as Florida, Nevada, Texas, or New Hampshire, where there is no state income tax. There are states that do not levy estate taxes, and there are federal exemptions you can explore that will help you save more money to pass to your children. I firmly believe that if you are retiring soon, think about legacy planning, or any type of planning to provide for your family. Know your options. Where you live and the costs associated with living there, specifically the costs that result from tax laws in your state can have a direct impact on your savings. Granted, you may not want to move away from your children, grandchildren, social organizations, or friends, but you should at least consider the advantages of relocating to a town that may have a lower tax rate. You might lose the cachet of a fancier town with a great school district—but why live somewhere with great schools if your children are grown? Take time to investigate your options.

As a financial planner, I often use the idea of "buckets" to illustrate sound budgeting. Bucket one is the money you will need for long-term care. Bucket two is the money that is going to pay for your daily living needs. Bucket three is the money you will need to travel, to spend on your hobbies, or to do whatever you enjoy. Lastly, there is bucket four, which is the money that is put in a trust, which you want to leave as a legacy to your children and/or charity. I find that this illustration helps clients gain a firm grasp of where their money is going, as well as provides a framework for where expenses might be reduced.

PLAN AHEAD FOR LONG-TERM CARE

The costs of long-term care can be devastating. The sooner you consider these costs and get insurance, the better. I recommend you contemplate purchasing insurance in your late fifties or early sixties; do not wait past these years. Get long-term health insurance while you are still healthy so that your rates will be lower. When couples tell me this type of insurance is cost prohibitive for both of them, I recommend they purchase at least one policy. In my experience, it is usually women who need long-term care insurance more than men. Why? The typical pattern is that the wife lives longer than the husband. She is available to care for her husband when he is sick. It is unlikely the husband will need a nursing home if his wife is well enough to care for him and if his care can be managed at home. When the husband passes away, the wife is left on her own. She could live another ten years or more, but when she gets sick, no one is with her to assist with her care. As a result, the wife should have some type of long-term care insurance. Today, long-term care policies are flexible. Policies can be purchased for both husband and wife by electing to have that option. If the husband does not exercise the policy, the remaining years can go to his wife. Ideally, you can buy two years on the husband and two years on the wife. If the husband never uses it, all of it goes to his wife, giving her four years of coverage. Insurance companies are analyzing needs and becoming more flexible with their offerings. There are even long-term care policies that have a death benefit. The death benefit payout is typically modest, but at least some of your money can go to your heirs in the event you die without using the policy for nursing-home care.

The unfortunate reality is that many insurance companies are no longer selling long-term care insurance. Unlike life insurance where policyholders lower their benefit or discontinue their coverage in their senior years, long-term care insurance policyholders hang onto their policies because over time the chances are greater that they will need long-term care.

Individuals with the resources to enter a high-end continuing care retirement community may feel better served with this option rather than purchase long-term care insurance. Continuing care retirement communities (CCRC) provide a continuum of care across assisted living, long-term care, and skilled care. This option is generally cost prohibitive for most. It requires a substantial deposit, which is often the sale price of one's home as well as a considerable monthly rental payment. The deposit is returned at a discount when the individual no longer lives at the facility. One of my client's lives in an upscale CCRC. She put down a significant deposit and spends a hefty $6,000 per month on her living expenses. This arrangement clearly isn't for everyone, but she can afford it, and she likes the peace of mind knowing if she experiences a health issue, she can transfer to an onsite acute-care bed. When this client told me of her desire to live in a CCRC nearly ten years ago, we did some planning to be sure she had enough assets to pay her monthly expenses. Today, she lives without concern knowing she can afford to stay there for the rest of her life.

Some seniors prefer the idea of staying at home, especially given the escalating cost of nursing-home care today. In the Northeast, assisted nursing-home care costs upward of $400 per day. Even when you have long-term care insurance paying $200 per day, you still must fund the remaining $200 per day from your savings. This scenario would have you paying about $73,000 a year for assisted care. Therefore, I tell my clients to create a bucket for this purpose. You don't have to fund the account with the full amount since you are not going into the nursing home today. We can perform calculations based on an expected rate of return over a specific time period to provide you with the amount needed today so that the account is fully funded in the future.

ADVANCE PLANNING AND THE FIVE-YEAR LOOK BACK

According to a Genworth study, the annual, national median cost for a private room in a nursing home facility was $100,375 in 2018. And that pales in comparison to the Northeast, where the median for a private room in a nursing home was $153,300 in Massachusetts[2] This could easily wipe out a lifetime of savings. There are a few ways to deal with this situation by doing some planning.

It is important to consider government regulations with respect to nursing home care. Here is what you need to know: Medicaid is a government-sponsored health insurance program funded by both the federal and state governments to provide care for people whose incomes fall below a certain level. Today, Medicaid is paying almost half of all skilled and long-term nursing-home bills. Why? The apparent reason is that our demographics are shifting; we have a growing, aging population in need of care. The not-so-obvious reason is that financially savvy people have been giving away their money and property in order to qualify for Medicaid coverage sooner than they would need. Medicaid planning has become a prevalent tool in estate planning, allowing those with means to pass some of their assets to their beneficiaries via a trust. The trust becomes an investment vehicle that can grow for the next generation.

In 2006, Congress enacted more stringent restrictions to limit these activities. The government extended the look-back period from three years to five years. The transfer of assets or gifts made prior to the five years from the date of application is not subject to penalties. Any transfers made during the five year period could result in a penalty extending the time in which you can apply for Medicaid assistance.

Let's assume my client is a seventy-nine-year-old widow or divorcee with considerable assets; I am going to recommend she speak with an elder care attorney. I have an obligation to educate her about asset protection planning. Trust set up and funding needs

---

2   Genworth 2018 Cost of Care Survey, conducted by CareScount, July 2018, https://www.genworth.com/aging-and-you/finances/cost-of-care.html

to be completed at least five years before she applies for Medicaid assistance. If she retains too many assets outside of her trust, she will not be Medicaid eligible.

On occasion, estate planning attorneys will recommend placing some of the assets into an irrevocable trust. Once assets are put in the irrevocable trust, they are no longer "yours." The assets now belong to the trust and are managed by the trustees. It is hard for people to sign off on this because they feel like they are giving away their savings. What I tell my clients is, "*You have two options: spend it on the nursing home or secure it for your heirs. Let me know where you would prefer the money to go.*" If you don't have enough funds to pay your expenses for skilled or long-term nursing home care, then those costs will be covered by Medicaid, and the trust will protect your assets for your children.

At the same time, I'm not saying move all your assets into a trust, and I also recommend people consider buying long-term care insurance when possible. The average stay in a nursing home, according to a study done in 2008 by the American Association for LTCI, is estimated at 3.7 years for females.[3] As reported by the CDC, from 2011 to 2012, some 67.7 percent of nursing-home patients were women, and 62.7 percent of home-health agency users were women.[4] If you have long-term care insurance that will pay somewhere around $150–$200 per day, then you can supplement the other $100–$150 per day out of assets that you kept outside of the trust. If you go beyond five years and you run out of money, then

---

3   "What Is the Probability You'll Need Long-Term Care? Is Long-Term Care Insurance a Smart Financial Move?", American Association for Long-Term Care Insurance, 2016, http://www.aaltci.org/long-term-care-insurance/learning-center/proba-bilitylong-term-care.php.

4   US Department of Health and Human Services, *Long Term Care Services in The United States: 2013 Overview*, http://www.cdc.gov/nchs/data/nsltcp/long_term_care_services_2013.pdf.

at least you protected some of your assets (by placing them in a trust five years prior to applying for Medicaid) for your children or charity. Seeking expert advice is imperative. I recommend anyone who has a loved one in need of assisted living meet with a qualified elder care attorney to discuss other options such as Pooled Trusts.

If you purchased a long-term policy, you could look at your other assets, and if you're sufficiently well-off, you might decide that you want to put a trust in place today, so you know a portion of your assets will be passed on to your children. It's a win-win situation because even if you remain healthy and independent, that money will not be included as part of your estate.

One of the primary concerns of a single parent is setting aside enough money for their descendant(s) in the event of their premature death. Think about it; your loved ones would be faced with paying your bills, your funeral expenses, potentially your mortgage, your legal fees, etc. While you may want your estate to pay for some of these expenses as a way to lower the value of the estate, recognize that your child will need access to your funds. There are creative ways to achieve this through account registrations thus avoiding the time it takes for probate to divvy up your assets. Remember, expenses start coming fast when there is a death, and your children are going to need to be able to access cash quickly. You can easily accomplish this by establishing a TOD (transfer on death) for investment accounts or a POD (pay on death) for your bank accounts. Request beneficiary designations on all your accounts so that your heir (designated beneficiary) can present a copy of your official death certificate to the institution and have the money moved to an accessible account. All this planning may seem intimidating, especially if you are not used to thinking in these terms. But, being prepared is not difficult, and it will save your loved ones some frustration and time while dealing with their loss.

Action Checklist

Chapter Two: Your Financial Checkup

- ☐ Gather information for a financial plan.

- ☐ Make your retirement wish list.

- ☐ Review spending— make a list of your discretionary spending vs. your necessity spending- do you need to make adjustments?

- ☐ Make SMART (Specific, Measurable, Attainable, Relevant, and Timely) buying decisions.

- ☐ Consider long-term care insurance and Medicaid planning.

- ☐ Place beneficiary designations on your accounts.

Chapter Three

"WHAT HAPPENS TO ME IF MY SPOUSE DIES?"

It is a scenario nobody wants to imagine or even think about, but it is all too common for women to lose their spouses. On average, women live longer than men. A study released by the CDC states that in 2015, women had a greater chance of outliving their spouse by 4.9 years.[5] This data has remained consistent for a number of years. It is a shattering experience: whether it happens suddenly or after a long illness, losing your spouse can leave you exhausted and paralyzed with grief.

There are the obvious items that must be addressed immediately at death, such as making funeral arrangements, notifying family and friends, placing an obituary in the local paper, and keeping a record of donations, flowers, and cards. If you and your loved one made plans other than a funeral, then keep to those expressed wishes. A friend of my family wanted to leave the world the same way she

---

5   Centers for Disease Control and Prevention, "Deaths: Final Data for 2015," https://www.cdc.gov/nchs/data/nvsr/nvsr66/nvsr66_06.pdf.

entered: no obituary, no funeral, no donations. This was her wish, and in true form, it was exactly what her husband did. Many of us have an opinion on what we would like, and it is best to express those wishes to all involved.

DON'T RUSH INTO ANYTHING

When it comes to making major decisions after immediate concerns have been handled, my best advice to someone who has just lost a partner is *do nothing*. It is difficult to place an exact time frame on how long to wait as we all process the passage from being married to widowed differently. Generally, I recommend a 6–12 month waiting period.

It's best to take the time to grieve and wait for the worst to pass. Unfortunately, not everyone has the ability to wait, as that depends on their finances. If your spouse was the breadwinner and you are strapped for money, I recommend you seek expert help to determine your options. It is never a good idea to make decisions when you are tired or stressed; do not rush into anything, even if children or others are urging you to take action. Focus on dealing with the day-to-day demands of paying your bills such as the mortgage, utilities, taxes and other regular expenses. I advise women to be cautious and speak with their attorney or executor before paying any of the deceased's expenses. If the value of the estate is high, for example, it would be best to have the estate pay the expenses to reduce the value of the estate. Estate taxes have changed due to governmental policies. It is best to be aware of the current legislation on this issue. It is also a good idea to re-title accounts, but this task can wait until the hardest times have passed.

FIND SUPPORT AND KEEP BUSY

I advise new widows to seek emotional support during their time of loss. There are therapists and bereavement groups often associated with hospices or churches where you can find a sympathetic ear and people who understand what it's like to lose a spouse. It is not uncommon to experience severe emotional swings, and being with people who understand and are able to relate can be quite comforting. Group settings are not for everyone—I would probably be one of those who would prefer to grieve alone—but many people find support from others tremendously helpful.

Staying busy can also be instrumental in dealing with a loss. I had a meeting with a client recently who told me, "*The one thing I make sure I do is to have one activity planned for every day.*" Having lost her husband a little over a month ago, she maintains daily activities that give her a reason to get up and get out of the house, and it requires her to function. She knows she is depressed, and she knows that she is not the same woman she used to be, but her activities help her to continue to engage with the world, even if she doesn't feel up to it on a particular day. So, it is helpful to do something, whether it is going to the movies, playing tennis or golf, playing cards, or just meeting someone for coffee. Sometimes it feels like you are just going through the motions, but those motions can keep you moving forward, one step at a time, one day at a time, toward healing.

It is also smart to take time before starting a new relationship. Even though loneliness can creep in, finding someone new so soon after a loss can be a rash choice that winds up being a wrong one. One of my clients jumped into a relationship three months after her husband passed away. She got remarried, and it wasn't the right choice. She was just too afraid of being alone, but she would have been far better off to have joined a support group where she could have met other women who were experiencing similar feelings. And it is worth mentioning here, distasteful as it is, there are predatory types out there who hone in on recent widows or widowers and take advantage of their vulnerability and their money.

GET YOUR PAPERWORK IN ORDER

If you have completed the task of gathering your financial information into a "just in case" file (as outlined in chapter 1), then the following steps should be straight forward. There are a few items that need attention due to legal matters. First of all, ask if the funeral home will be able to supply you with certified copies of the death certificate. Typically I recommend 10-15 copies. You should also instruct the estate executor or attorney to begin an inventory of the decedent's property and to start the probate process if necessary. If no executor is named, a judge will usually appoint the surviving spouse. This process needs to be completed within ninety days from the date of death. Your "just in case" file should have all the information you need to start transitioning assets. Additionally, you will need to be prepared to file taxes without your spouse. If your spouse's death occurred before April 15, your tax filing obligations do not change due to a death. Unfortunately, this cannot be postponed.

After a couple of months have passed, it is time to sit down and look at your finances. If you are uncomfortable with the person your spouse was using as an accountant or advisor, take the time to find someone you like to work with. More women are registered as financial advisors today than ever before. You are not obligated to stay with the same advisor, broker, custodian, or financial institution; accounts and investments are transferable. Find someone whose advice you can trust and who can help you through the process.

EVALUATE YOUR ASSETS

When a spouse passes away, the surviving spouse must reevaluate his or her financial situation, which may or may not require a change in lifestyle. It's important to reassess your means—to evaluate the situation and ask, "*What does my income stream look like? How will my expenses change?*"

If your Social Security benefit was less than your spouse's or was a spousal benefit, then you will need to reapply with the Social Security Administration to get his full benefit. If the deceased spouse had a pension with a survivorship option, you need to contact the pension company to have the payout changed; the same is true if your spouse had a 401(k) plan. If your spouse had some other type of plan, then you need to get in touch with the plan administrator to learn about your options. Ask if you can resume the plan, or find out if it has to be disbursed into an IRA to you. If the 401(k) needs to be terminated, the sooner that is done, the better. If something happened to you as the beneficiary, it would be advantageous if that money was in an IRA with your children listed as beneficiaries so they could have the option of creating a tax-deferred, inherited IRA upon your passing.

To assess all your available assets, you must review your financial records thoroughly. This is when having that "just in case" file becomes so important: if you know where your money is coming from, and how much money you have, you will be in a position to begin making appropriate financial plans.

If financial records are not organized, you will have to dig into your spouse's records and research everything to locate all the assets so that you can establish an income stream. It is smart to write notes directly on documents when you have them in hand, noting when and whom you spoke with and recording short descriptions of the conversation. For example: "Called on this date, spoke with this person, the account was moved to . . ." Be sure to record the nature and purpose of the call. You should take the time to do this because years later, you'll look at these papers again and think, *Oh, this might be worth something* and then waste time just spinning your wheels to find out the assets were already transferred into your name. People hesitate to write notes on documents because they are afraid they will void something if they write on it. That is not the case—you can even write on a stock certificate. It's not going to make it null and void. So, take good notes on documents because a year from now, you are not going to remember the conversation. Some clients have a notebook that they keep just for this purpose, and they can consult it days, weeks, months, or even years later when questions arise. At some point in time, you will come across the document again and perhaps then you will say, *"Oh, I took care of this; it's all set. Now is the time to shred this paperwork."*

WHO ARE THE BENEFICIARIES?

It is important to consider your beneficiaries, especially after a life-changing event. If your marriage to your recently deceased spouse was a second or subsequent marriage, your spouse's previous wife might have rights to some of your money. Not only is it important to know what assets are yours, but it is also important to know the beneficiaries on the accounts. Are the funds directed to you or to the previous wife or a child from that marriage?

Typically, with a 401(k) plan or a corporate-sponsored plan, the wife is always the primary beneficiary unless she elects not to be. The only exception would be if you and your husband were not married when he initially began the plan, and he subsequently neglected to designate you as his beneficiary after your marriage. It is not up to the administrator of the plan to say, "*Now that you are married. You need to change your retirement beneficiary form.*" You must be responsible for updating your beneficiaries. Obviously, if you experience any life-altering events such as a marriage or a divorce, you may be more inclined to look at your documents and to make sure that your beneficiaries are up-to-date. I cannot emphasize enough that you should periodically review your beneficiary designations on all assets.

REBALANCING YOUR BUDGET

Rebalancing your budget is typically required after the death of a spouse. As the survivor, you need to consider the income and expense equation. Maybe your spending has decreased, and you could be putting some money aside in a savings vehicle instead of just leaving it in a checking account. If you are receiving distributions from your IRA prior to age seventy and a half, and it is more money than you need, request to have it decreased. Why pay taxes on the money you are not using?

If you have a child in college when your spouse dies, and your spouse was the breadwinner, find out if you are able to apply for financial aid. Call the financial aid department at your child's college and consider all available options.

Do you have to sell your home? Perhaps you could afford to keep your home when your husband was alive, but now that the income flow has been reduced, maintaining the home may be too expensive. This becomes more of an issue when you are dealing with children who are still in the local school system because you do not necessarily want to uproot them. However, if you live in a town where there are no significantly cheaper homes, moving to a new town and transferring your children to a new school system may be your best financial decision. This is a time to consult with a financial planner—seek someone who has the qualifications to advise and assist with these types of issues. If there are savings put away, you might be able to stay afloat for several years, until the last child graduates, before selling your home. If your spouse had life insurance and/or if you have mortgage insurance, that proactive planning can make the difference between maintaining your current lifestyle or downsizing to a very different one.

WHAT ARE YOUR OPTIONS REGARDING YOUR SPOUSE'S 401(K)?

If the participant of a 401(k) plan dies, the surviving beneficiary will either have to take the account and roll it over into an IRA or take disbursements from the account for a defined period of time. If you are the widow of a participant of a 401(k) plan, I highly recommend you call the plan administrator and ask how to roll it over into an IRA for yourself and then assign your beneficiaries as you deem appropriate. You shouldn't wait for months to contact the 401(k) administrator—this is something that should be addressed sooner rather than later.

For example, if you have children, it is best to roll over the assets to an IRA rollover account soon so that you can label the children as beneficiaries. The IRA rollover gives your children the option to take a full distribution and pay the tax consequences or to place their share of the funds in an inherited IRA to continue to reap the benefits of a tax-deferred account in the event of your death. If your assets are kept in a 401(k) plan and you passed away, your children may not have the opportunity to roll the money out into an inherited

IRA. The company plan may require they take a full disbursement immediately or over five years, thus causing a taxable event.

Knowing the plan options is paramount to maximize the benefit of what your 401(k) plan will be able to provide you and your family. IRAs allow beneficiaries to decide what they would like to do with their inheritance. It is important to note that if a beneficiary elects to move IRA funds into an Inherited IRA, the recipient will need to take required minimum distributions prior to age seventy and a half.

REVISIT YOUR WILL AND TRUST

I am frequently amazed when I learn that many otherwise responsible people don't have a will or a trust. It is one of those "*Yeah, I'll get to it*" items, but often, you never do. Let's say there is no will, there is no trust, and there are no beneficiaries on the accounts; everything is in the owner's name. In this case, the succession of solely owned property that does not have a designated beneficiary will depend upon state law. Every state has intestate succession laws that divvy out solely owned property. However, the general rule is that spouses, registered domestic partners, and blood relatives inherit the assets under intestate succession law. Knowing and understanding your state laws is important. Taking the time to designate heirs on accounts or creating a will or a trust can avoid the uncertainty of inheritance. After a life-altering event, also remember to review and if necessary modify your legal documents, so that they reflect your current situation and your wishes.

In addition, after the death of your spouse, you may need to revise your healthcare documents. Typically, your spouse is your designated power of attorney or agent on your healthcare proxy; therefore, you will need to appoint someone else. While you are doing this, you might want to reevaluate your advanced directive. As you may recall from chapter 1, the advanced directive specifies what actions you want taken for your health if you are no longer able to make decisions for yourself.

If your spouse has left behind significant hospital bills, you should consider contacting the hospital's patient services financial office and asking for a reduction to keep those accounts from going into collections. This is not an unusual request or anything to fear; there are representatives that will work with you to reduce your bill and will offer a courtesy adjustment to settle your balance, especially upon death. Doctors' offices may also be willing to work with you in this regard.

Upon the death of your spouse, make sure that the deed to your home is re-titled in your name. The cars, boats, and other titled assets also need to be transferred to your name.

It's a good idea to request several certified copies of your late spouse's death certificate. Typically, you need one for every institution you need to contact to change registration. If there is a 401(k) plan, you will need a copy for that. If there are multiple IRAs with different custodians—for example, an IRA at a brokerage firm and one at the local bank—you will need one for each institution. In the event your spouse had a life insurance policy, the insurance company will also require a copy. Your funeral home can supply these to you, usually for a nominal fee. As a general rule of thumb, estimate that you will need ten to fifteen certificates; I advise my clients that it is better to have more than you think you will need rather than having to go back to request additional copies. Many clients whose spouses have passed away find even small to-do items, such as returning to the funeral home to be painful reminders of their loss, so cover your bases as much as possible to avoid unnecessary heartache and headache at a later date.

CANCEL AUTOMATIC PAYMENTS AND POLICIES NO LONGER IN USE

Remember to notify your home, medical, dental, auto, disability and long term care insurance companies of your husbands passing. It is important to know what automatic withdrawals are coming out of your accounts to pay bills. If, for example, your husband was paying $200 per month for his health or dental insurance policy, call your bank to stop the payments. There may also be monthly automated deductions for an automobile insurance policy that should be canceled once his car is no longer in use. If your husband had business-related insurance, such as a physician's malpractice insurance policy, speak with the insurance agent to determine if you can cancel the policy and get a prorated refund. If your husband had a professional license, you should have the license terminated as well. If a father and son had the same name, the son should make sure that his records aren't affected by his father's death.

Making funeral arrangements can be overwhelming; while there is much to coordinate, remember to consider where donations in lieu of flowers can be sent when preparing the obituary. If your loved one was in hospice at the end of life, you might want to direct donations in his name to that organization—but perhaps he had another charity or organization that was more meaningful to him over a longer term. If so, consider directing donations to that cause. If he was a devoted library user or volunteered at the local food pantry, it might be more appropriate to support these interests in his honor. Make a lovely tribute to his memory and reflect on what he cared about during his life.

Dealing with the death of a spouse is possibly one of the most challenging events you will experience during your lifetime. Know that it does get better; be prudent, don't be in a hurry, and don't let anyone rush you toward making any immediate decisions or changes. Find a good professional advisor to help you assess your financial standing and to assist you with planning for your future.

Action Checklist

Chapter Three: "What Happens to Me If My Husband Dies?"

☐ Call your husband's 401(K) Administrator; ask about rollover company-sponsored plans.

☐ Review automatic payments on bank accounts to avoid making double payments.

☐ Change registration of financial accounts.

☐ Set up new beneficiaries on accounts and life insurance/annuity policies.

☐ Change registration on the deed to your home and title of your automobiles and other valuable assets.

☐ Contact insurance companies to notify them of your spouse's death (e.g., auto, life, long -term care, home).

Chapter Four

"WHAT WILL HAPPEN IF I DIVORCE?"

Like death, divorce puts you on an emotional roller coaster. Nobody goes into a marriage thinking it will end in divorce. If your marriage has been unhappy, divorce provides you with some sense of relief, but it is still a profoundly difficult transition. For many women, especially those who are insecure about their financial future, there is danger in making emotion-driven decisions that will put their future in jeopardy, particularly early in the divorce process.

If you decide to move ahead with a divorce, or if you get served divorce papers, the first thing you would likely do is look for an attorney. You might shop around and meet with three or four firms, then select the attorney who makes you feel most comfortable. Make sure you understand the process you are choosing for your divorce because you have options. Historically, divorce was done via litigation, but times are changing, and the process is evolving. Today, there are three methods commonly used to consummate a divorce: collaborative, mediation, and litigation. No matter which method you select, it is important to know the fundamentals of how your financial division is viewed by the state. In the past, often attorneys would direct the process and make recommendations for the division of assets. Your attorney would have you sign papers, and upon your faithful execution of the divorce agreement, your divorce would be finalized—possibly without you fully realizing what you agreed to. Unfortunately, I have witnessed some poorly devised division of assets when divorcées see me for consultation.

A woman's unfavorable divorce settlement may be due to a lack of knowledge of future financial needs. Most women leave all aspects of their divorce to be managed by their attorney. They neglect to seek the advice of a Certified Divorce Financial Analyst (CDFA™). The CDFA performs an analysis of current living expenses, income, and future demands to evaluate the long-term cash flow needs. This analysis shows how the distribution of assets will affect the living conditions of the parties involved.

Signing papers and trying to get through the process as quickly as possible is understandable—divorce is stressful and often unpleasant. When I went through my own divorce, I was getting only two or three hours of sleep each night. There are so many moving parts and you can't possibly handle them all, and then when you add sleep deprivation on top of it, there comes a time where you may shut down and decide, *"I just want it done."* When the dust settles, once you are able to sleep and have a clear mind, you may question what you did. During the negotiations, you felt ending the process was what you needed to do, but upon reflection, you may wish you gave more thought to the decisions that were made.

DON'T GIVE AWAY THE FARM

One of the best recommendations I can make regarding your division of assets in divorce proceedings is to consult with someone in addition to your attorney. Find a neutral party who can analyze the proposal and put the divorce into numbers. By determining what you both own, what you are both making, and then modeling an ideal division of assets. What I have typically seen during a divorce, is fatigue and exhaustion. Too often, rather than continuing to fight over assets, a woman will simply throw up her hands and say, "*He can have it.*" At that moment, she may not really care about that item as she is operating from a place of just wanting the whole thing over and done. But the fact is that, often, she is giving away an asset for which she should be compensated.

A family friend and her husband had an extensive wine collection that consisted of hundreds of bottles they had collected over many years. Her knowledge of the value of the different wines, which varied from not so valuable to extremely valuable, was limited. When they were quarreling over the collection's disposition, she said, "*You know what? Just come and take whatever wines you want.*" So, he came in and took all the expensive bottles and left her with the least valuable. She did not realize that she was giving away her assets—she just let him walk away with about $10,000 worth of their prized wines. She failed to realize that the value of the wine was not being accounted for; it was being lost. Valuable collections that may only be of interest to your husband should not be overlooked when considering a division of assets. Get the valuables appraised by an expert. Know what they are worth. I am not talking about penny-pinching but about substantial sums of money that the wife winds up leaving on the table because she is not taking the time to get the actual value for these types of assets. Sure, if you don't care about the wine collection, let him take all the wine. And if you care more about the furniture or if you care more about having hard cash, say, "*Here, you can take all the wine. But I'm going to offset it by keeping what we have in the savings account.*"

I worked with a woman whose husband had a coin collection. He kept saying, "*Well, that is my asset,*" but it was something that was purchased over the lifetime of the marriage. Because he claimed the coin collection as personal assets, she felt she couldn't bring it up in the divorce. Was she compensated for that elsewhere? No. Clearly the coins should have been declared on the division of asset list.

Let's discuss the family house. It comes down to knowing about the asset, what it is worth, and how you'll be impacted, whether you choose to keep it or give it up. The wife might think, *I can't afford this. I can't stay here. I'm going to walk away from the house.* Or she may insist on keeping the marital home when she apparently cannot afford it. It is the emotional turmoil that she is going through that causes her to make bad decisions.

On the other hand, she might decide to sell the house once she finalizes her divorce. What she may not anticipate is the unintended tax implications of that decision. When making these types of decisions, you must ask yourself, *Is there a capital gain from the sale of the home? Would it have been better to sell the house while you were married?* I remember a case where there was a $300,000 gain on the house, and as an individual taxpayer, my client only had a $250,000 exclusion that she could use against that gain, so she was going to have a capital gains tax on the $50,000. If she had sold the home prior to finalizing the divorce, the capital gain would have been eliminated. As joint owners of the home, the husband would also have had an exclusion of $250,000, so together they would have had a $500,000 exclusion for capital gains.

INVEST IN PROFESSIONAL
VALUATIONS OF YOUR ASSETS

Often, when people are getting divorced, especially if the wife has been a stay-at-home mom, she may be at a loss wondering how she will pay for services that determine value. Many times, I advise women to speak to their attorney. If they have not officially filed for divorce, they can use funds in the joint account. Sometimes, women don't see the money in the joint account as their asset, but it is, and they should use that money to get valuations. It is odd how often men will feel so much more justified in taking what they see as "theirs." While this might be due to the way you have been brought up, that shouldn't stand in the way of an equitable split of assets. If you have reason to believe that your marriage is going to end, then start to put money aside to pay for professional fees. To do this, you may want to open a bank account in your own name at a different bank.

Divorce can bring out the worst in people in terms of the emotions you experience—and the financial wrangling that ensues. I have personally seen cases in which one partner—the one who's planning to leave the marriage—systematically begins to secretly set aside assets, with the intent of hiding them from the spouse. They put money into a safety-deposit box or a hidden account. Sometimes, they give money to relatives to hold for them. There is also the private business owner who primarily runs a cash business and has a tremendous opportunity to hide assets, and if your spouse is in that position and you suspect he may have had this planned for some time, it might be worthwhile to hire a forensic accountant. Many people who run a cash business have two sets of books: one for the IRS and one with the real profit numbers.

When you hire a forensic accountant, that person is looking at your tax returns. Yes, this includes looking at the bank—but if that money is never hitting the bank, then that forensic accountant is trained to look at your lifestyle to uncover discrepancies.

Sometimes the husband is just a cheap guy, and the lifestyle doesn't reflect reality. For instance, I had a client whose husband kept her in the dark regarding anything that had to do with the household finances. My client thought their total savings amounted to $100,000. She always watched her nickels and dimes because he made her think they were skating on the edge. When they got divorced, she found out that they had a lot of money—more than $2 million in savings! He had been lying to her all those years.

The basis of this book should start sounding more and more familiar; know what you own.

SEEK FINANCIAL ADVICE

Women should depend on their attorneys when it comes to divorce, right? Yes, when it comes to the law. However, there are many more professionals that have developed over the years that have gained traction because of the balance they bring to the table. While attorneys may be part of the process, they most certainly should not be used exclusively when seeking a divorce. I have had a few clients whose attorneys felt that it was best for the woman to retain qualified assets (tax-deferred retirement account funds) so that she would have retirement assets—but the attorneys were not considering her cash flow. When they were dividing up the assets, they were pressing for more of the 401(k) plan money and less of the joint assets that were sitting in the bank.

Why is this problem? Number one, the money in the bank is tax-free. The money in the 401(k) is pretax dollars. For every dollar you have in a bank account, you must match that with more dollars from the 401(k) account. For example, if you are in the 25 percent tax bracket, the value of $1.00 is equivalent to $1.33 in the 401(k).

If you or your attorney is arguing for a larger share of the 401(k) plan, and you do not have the adequate cash flow to manage your current spending, you are going to have to dip into that retirement account prematurely. This means that the IRA that was there for your retirement won't necessarily be there when you need it. You may have to draw it down to cover your current living expenses. Additionally, if you are younger than fifty-nine and a half years old, you now have the 10 percent penalty to consider every time you take a distribution from the account. This just compounds the issue.

When you consult with a financial advisor or someone who is certified to do a financial analysis, the analyst will look at all the factors. As a Certified Divorce Financial Analyst, I have been trained and given tools to draw up models. I create plans. I look at how everything is arranged and I consider all assets so that I am in a position to give the best advice. I consider how best to cover your living expenses, plus I determine how to plan ahead for your retirement. Your attorney will work out the alimony and the child support, but don't expect her or him to be an expert in the division of assets. Even in the case of an amicable divorce, one in which both parties are trying to do the right thing, you can end up in a financial pit if the assets are improperly divided. While both parties may determine that the wife and children should remain living in the family home, if that is not possible or if that is going to strain the budget, it is better to know that early in the process and to come up with a different plan. Children are resilient. They will end up adapting to a new home. We often try to shelter our children from divorce and the consequences that ensue. I personally feel that if you can live in the same town, in a cheaper or rented house, you and your children will be far better off than you would be struggling, trying to make ends meet living in the same family home.

Although you may be awarded a large alimony payment, and you may feel confident that you are able to afford the home, you should know that your ex-husband can take you back to court to modify the payment, especially if he becomes unable to afford the alimony. If you've made your financial decisions based on your expectation of getting a certain amount of money per month, your situation could substantially change if your alimony is lowered. It is better to know what you are capable of affording and what is feasible and sustainable.

Child support guidelines are posted on most state official websites, and most of these sites have programmed calculators to help you know where you might stand after a divorce. If you are thinking of getting a divorce you can input the information and know ahead of time your state's child support guidelines or what type of alimony you might be able to receive.

Certified Divorce Financial Analysts project forecasts and run models; they are looking at the lifespan of each client and questioning what the situation will look like twenty years from now and beyond. Does John Doe end up with $6 million and Jane Doe end up in bankruptcy? And if that is at a fifty-fifty division of assets, can we change the division so that Jane isn't in poverty?

WHAT ARE YOUR OPTIONS FOR DIVORCE?

As mentioned earlier, the process of divorce is changing. In the past, a woman would hire an attorney—most likely a litigator. Today, however, couples have more options than ever before when it comes to filing for a divorce. Currently, as mentioned above, there are three options: mediated divorce, collaborative divorce, and litigated divorce.

In an amicable divorce, typically the husband and wife have decided that they are not happy together and that they would be better off dissolving the marriage. Sometimes relationships do not work out soon after marriage and other times couples stay married many years for the sake of their children, but at some point, they both decide to dissolve the marriage. In this situation, mediation may be the best option. Mediation usually tends to be less expensive, but understand that you are not getting advice when you are going through mediation. In mediation, when there is something that is stopping the process from moving forward, the mediator is there to facilitate and move the procedure forward. If you have agreed to go through mediation, it is very important that both parties know the financials and where they stand. In addition, I recommend you hire an attorney to review the final draft to ensure it is what you want.

I worked with a couple going through a divorce, the husband knew more than the wife about their finances. The three of us sat down and went through their financials together. I gave them the best advice possible and established a fair division of assets. The mediator wasn't helping them; the husband was trying to control the whole process, and the wife was going along with it because she was the one who wanted to leave the marriage to be with a former boyfriend. Her guilt over what she was doing was driving the decisions she was making on the division of assets, and she gave away more than she should have, against my advice.

That is why I warn people to be careful when it comes to mediation, you must know what you want, and any division of assets must be fair. It is vital to have a financial expert look through the assets. A mediator isn't going to provide advice on how to do that.

Not all mediators are attorneys; anybody can go through mediation training and hang out a shingle. Make sure you have a mediator who is an attorney; otherwise, they may not understand all the legal ramifications of your agreement. And even if your mediator is an attorney, do seek out a financial advisor as well. Make sure your finances are going to be divided amicably and properly between you.

Collaborative divorce has become more popular. The collaborative process brings together a team of professionals to handle the many aspects of divorce. The premise behind the collaborative approach is to provide both parties with support and guidance to avoid going to court. You, the client, select which professionals you want on your team. Typically, the team will consist of an attorney and a divorce coach who work together to assist in your divorce. During the process, other specialists will be consulted as needed. Ultimately, you and your partner drive the divorce, and the process allows you to negotiate a settlement out of court. If during this process there is a breakdown in the negotiations, the coach steps in like a mediator to get you over that rough spot. The coach might say, "Let's look at the problem. Let's put it up on the board and figure out a way to work around this so that we can get you both through this divorce in a healthy manner." This is a relatively new approach that has come into play within the last seven years. It can help the divorce process move more smoothly and keep people out of expensive court hearings.

Lastly, there is a litigated divorce. This is the style of divorce that is familiar to most people. Each party hires an attorney to argue their case. If an agreement cannot be reached, then the matter will go to court, and a judge will make a ruling for the parties. This approach to divorce is best used when a partner is unwilling to cooperate or if there are abuse issues involved. The attorneys oversee the process, and the divorcing couple relies solely on their respective lawyers. It should be noted that most litigation cases never go to trial and are settled out of court.

KNOW YOUR ASSETS

As mentioned earlier, every state is different in how it defines marital assets, and when you are going through a divorce, you need to know what counts. Research the general guidelines for your state if you are thinking of filing for divorce. Your best bet for good advice would be your state's official website. There you will also find information on your state's laws regarding alimony and child support.

There are nine different states right now that are community property states. If you live in a community property state, when you come to the marriage, whatever you come with is yours, and whatever your spouse comes with remains his so long as you do not commingle assets. Whatever you built together during the marriage is both of yours. The income you make is considered a marital asset, so the items you buy while married are marital property. In divorce, a community property state will split all marital assets fifty-fifty. In addition, if the assets you bring to the marriage are commingled, they could become marital assets. If the separate property can no longer be distinguished from the marital assets, it will become part of the divorce settlement. However, all separate property that has not been commingled remains separate and is not divided in a divorce. It is important to know how property is classified. Knowing what your state recognizes as separate or marital property is essential. Doing your homework and doing some planning may prevent headaches and tremendous financial hardships.

Living in fear with little knowledge puts you in a weak position. If you do your research, you will become more informed and better prepared to take control. Being informed will empower you to move forward confidently. A financial planner can help you crunch the numbers, so you will know what to expect later in life, and that is valuable information.

One problem many stay-at-home moms face when getting a divorce is the expectation that they're going to have to refinance the house in order to buy out their husband's share. It is of vital importance that your attorney understands your situation, it is difficult to get a mortgage today, and with no job history, income history, or credit in your name, it can be impossible to qualify for a loan. Leading up to the great recession of 2008, anyone could get a mortgage without any type of asset verification or income verification, but that has changed. Today, you must prove that you have the income to support a mortgage. When dealing with a divorce, the bank will generally refinance the home after six to twelve months of regular alimony and/or child support payments have been made. At that point, one may be able to qualify. That is why it is important to make sure alimony and child support are enough to qualify for home refinancing. Don't neglect the vital step of getting a credit report done before your settlement; you may have significant debts for which you have some liability—a credit card your husband may use that you don't know about, with a massive, racked-up bill for instance. One of the most important, immediate steps you should take is to remove your name off any joint credit cards for which you are not the primary holder. Accordingly, remove your spouse from any account which you are the primary credit card holder. If your spouse has debts, make sure that those debts are discussed during the process of the division of assets so that you can argue for relief of at least some of the debt. Speak with the credit card companies to know your options. If you close too many accounts, you could create a negative effect on your credit rating.

Divorce is exhausting, scary, and depressing. There will be times when all you want is out—and those are the times when you need to be the most prudent and the slowest to act. Don't sign away anything without understanding the ramifications of your decisions. *Don't* give away assets to speed up the process. Protect yourself through the process by hiring a financial expert who can help you make the best decisions as you go through this difficult and confusing process. If you feel there is blame on your part for the divorce, you have to let that go. Know your rights. Separate yourself from the emotions of guilt and fear which can push you in the wrong direction.

DOS	DON'TS
• Do seek legal assistance.	• Don't argue or criticize your spouse in front of the children.
• Do gather financial information.	
• Do communicate with your soon-to-be ex.	• Don't use your children as messengers.
• Do work out a parenting plan for the children.	• Don't withhold visitation from your spouse.
• Do seek financial assistance with a CDFA™.	• Don't burden your children with your troubles.
• Do be honest.	
• Do put the children first.	• Don't just "wing it"; have a plan!
• Do have a plan.	• Don't go it alone.
• Do take some time out for yourself.	• Don't focus on the small stuff.
• Do get some sleep. (This might be the hardest thing to do.)	• Don't lose your cool.
	• Don't make rash decisions.

UPDATE YOUR LEGAL DOCUMENTS

Once the divorce is over, you will need to make changes to all your legal documents (e.g., wills, trusts, medical directives, etc.). Similar to if your husband dies, you need to change beneficiaries, review insurance policies, and change the registration on your car, home and other assets.

Action Checklist

Chapter Four: "What Will Happen If I Divorce?"

- ☐ Become educated: attend divorce seminars, research your state's divorce guidelines, interview attorneys and financial divorce experts.

- ☐ Know your marital and personal assets (make an inventory list).

- ☐ Check your credit rating.

- ☐ Remove your spouse on all credit cards where he is a secondary user. Remove yourself from credit cards where you are a secondary user.

- ☐ If you do not have your own credit card, get one.

- ☐ Learn about the various ways to get a divorce.

- ☐ Know what your monthly expenses are so you can budget for them.

- ☐ Put aside enough money to pay for legal and professional services—even if you think you have enough, get more!

- ☐ Be prepared to negotiate for what is yours regardless of who wants the divorce.

- ☐ If the stress is getting to you, find a way to relax (meditation, yoga, a hobby).

- ☐ Keep a notebook of questions and answers (this is a long strenuous process, and you will not remember everything).

Chapter Five

LOVE AND REMARRIAGE

As joyous as new love and remarriage can be, they can also bring a host of challenges and changes to your financial situation. Go into remarriage with your eyes open. Everyone wants to believe their marriage will last forever, and no one likes to think about other possibilities while they're in the throes of love. Even though the idea of signing a prenuptial agreement—more commonly referred to as a "prenup"—may sound terribly unromantic, it is prudent for both parties to work with an attorney to establish one, particularly as it relates to the flow of assets in the event of your death.

If there are considerable assets, you should also see an attorney. Setting up a trust assures that your partner can access a portion of the trust assets, in the event of your death. Upon, your spouse's death, the trust assets can be passed to your children. At this stage of life when you may have amassed substantial assets, you have to be prepared and consider how things might play out in the future.

THE RULES ON ASSETS DIFFER

Depending on the state where you reside, the assets you bring into a marriage may remain your assets after divorce or they may not. In the state of Connecticut, for instance, everything is a marital asset as soon as you say, "*I do.*" In the Commonwealth of Massachusetts, what you bring to the marriage is separate property. Any assets accumulated after the marriage, belongs to both parties. For example, if you lived in Massachusetts and you came to the marriage with assets totaling $500,000, and during the marriage, the assets grew to $700,000, it could be argued that $200,000 of that account belongs to both you and your husband. If you live in Connecticut, the whole $700,000 is the property of both parties. Massachusetts law allows a judge to divide both marital and separate property in any manner that seems fair. When you are dealing with an equitable division of assets, every state has its own way of dividing them. If you had a prenuptial in place and had a discussion with your spouse about ownership ahead of time, and you both agreed to it, then you have minimized any tension or stress that could ensue regarding those funds going forward.

UPDATE YOUR IMPORTANT PAPERS

Many people do not consider all the little changes that need to take place when they remarry. If you have a will, trust, or beneficiaries, you need to revisit those agreements and make changes if appropriate. While you may love your new spouse very much, if you have an employer-sponsored 401(k) or an IRA and you want 100 percent going to your spouse if you die, does it revert back to your children if your spouse passes away after you? How do you make sure that it does? The fact is, once your 401(k) or IRA is bequeathed to your spouse it stops there. Unless your wishes about the contingent beneficiaries are written into a trust, or in a prenuptial agreement, there is no guarantee that your children will get any of that money. Therefore, you must revisit your legal documents to ensure they are up-to-date and will guarantee your assets are divided in accordance with your wishes.

Just recently, one of my clients passed away. Most of her assets were either in a joint account or else designated to her husband. This was a second marriage for both of them. Even though I had requested they see an attorney and put their assets into a trust, they felt that their estate was not large enough to require an attorney and that their mutual trust in each other to do the right things upon either of their deaths was sufficient. Well, the wife passed away, and then a few months later, the husband died. Because of state law, the husband's children from a previous marriage got everything—and her children received nothing, even though most of the assets were hers. Her children can try to contest the law, but the fact of the matter is the husband died without a will, so the matter will go through probate. It is possible the children could hire an attorney and contest the state showing that the assets were their mother's. There is a chance they could get some of the assets, but they will have to fight for it, and pay a fair amount in attorney and court fees to get what is rightfully theirs. If the parents had their affairs in order at the onset, then this type of effort would be avoided.

That is why it is vital that you change your will, your trust, and/ or your beneficiaries, and update your documents so that what you want to happen, will happen. Do not count on your spouse to make it right after you die because chances are it is not going to be done correctly.

MAKE APPROPRIATE CHANGES TO
YOUR INSURANCE POLICIES

If you have life insurance policies, should you change them? Sometimes people don't make an adjustment; if they have gone through a divorce and are in their second marriage, they will simply leave their life insurance benefits to their children and leave the new spouse the IRA assets. Why? Because life insurance can transfer tax-free to the children, and IRA assets can transfer tax-deferred to the spouse. If there are limited assets involved, it might also make sense to have another life insurance policy for the current spouse.

I advise my clients to work through these issues together. Both parties should feel that the resolution is equitable. Ideally, a couple should make it perfectly clear to each other what assets each of them brings to the marriage, before tying the knot. There should be clear decisions about the distribution of assets after death as well. Many of my clients have appreciated my insistence regarding this matter; they were glad they hammered out the details ahead of the wedding, thus avoiding worry, misunderstanding, and hurt feelings.

A PRENUPTIAL CAN DETER PROBLEMS
BEFORE THEY HAPPEN

Another client of mine who has a child with special needs went through a nasty divorce. After some time, my client started dating and soon told me she found the love of her life. "*Be careful,*" I said. "*You don't want to go into the second marriage so quickly just because you think you are in love. Make sure that this is what you really want, and make sure that you are protected.*"

Her prenuptial agreement listed all her assets, and her wishes for the distribution of her assets in the event of her death. She was glad she did. She laid it all out on the table and said to her fiancé, "*If you want to marry me, this is the deal. I'm not forcing you to sign it. It's up to you.*" Periodically, he would come back with recommendations from his attorney, and she would say, "*No, this is non-negotiable. This is what I'm offering.*" She was smart; she entered into the new marriage honestly and he was not coerced. She planned carefully, taking time to be sure everything was covered. The couple worked on the agreement for at least six or seven months before marrying, so there was no question of duress; either he signed off, or they were not getting married. It was done up front with full disclosure. At the time you marry, you are in love, and everything is happy and rosy—but those who are prepared will end up in a much better place down the road than those who go into it without thinking ahead.

Don't be fooled into believing prenups are only for the wealthy; for those who have fewer assets, I think a prenuptial is *more* important because there is not that much money to go around. If you want your children to receive their inheritance or if you want to ensure your separate property remains yours in case of a divorce, you need a prenuptial agreement.

How should you go about drafting a prenuptial? In my opinion, the best way is to hire an attorney to assist you. Attorney fees range anywhere from $200 to $500 per hour, depending on where you live. But a prenuptial can also be done over the dinner table. I know of one couple who drafted their prenuptial on a napkin, and they both signed it. Sounds crazy—but it held up in court. I do think it is best if both parties work with an attorney to resolve any issues. Ideally, there should be room for a little give and take, as there may be questions that one of you has not considered.

The most important aspect to remember with a prenuptial is not to conceal anything. All assets must be disclosed. One of my clients discovered during her divorce that her husband had not fully disclosed his assets when he presented the prenuptial, and as a result, she ended up with a lot more than she expected because the prenuptial was not valid. Her attorney was able to prove there was not full and fair disclosure of assets. Thus, it became a normal divorce proceeding where she received an equitable division of assets.

Remember that debts too must be disclosed when drawing up a prenuptial. A good friend of mine remarried and only after the marriage found out how much debt her new spouse carried. She learned to deal with it, but it was quite a shock. Had she insisted on a prenuptial, the agreement could have denoted that his debt would remain his alone.

A prenuptial is essential if you have minor children. Minor children cannot inherit assets; you must name a custodian to inherit your assets on your child's behalf, so when you are filling out beneficiary forms, you must remember you cannot designate minor children as benefactors. When I went through my divorce, my son was nine years old. After the divorce, I reestablished my beneficiaries, labeling my sister as a custodian for my son so that the designation would not be thrown back to the courts as an invalid beneficiary because he was not lawfully able to take receipt of assets. Most people do not understand that if you have a minor child and you want to pass assets on to that child, you must designate a custodian to handle the assets until the child comes of age. If you are getting divorced, you may not want the custodian to be your former spouse. It is important to have someone you can trust, someone that you know isn't going to take the money for themselves. In addition, it is important to let your new spouse know where he stands; review his responsibilities with him, and explain what assets will be available to him should something happen to you. While it is prudent to get your beneficiary paperwork in order, do not rush into changing things— and if you have a spouse who is urging you to change your beneficiaries, you must stop and ask why.

There are a few other aspects of prenups that I think people should know. First, a prenuptial should be in writing. Second, it should be executed voluntarily, with no pressure. Third, there should be full disclosure from both parties regarding assets and debts. Last, a prenup cannot be coerced; you must give the person time to consider the terms. Establishing a prenup takes work; it is not something that should be brought up at the eleventh hour. Prepare your prenup months before you remarry. If your fiancée signs just two days before your marriage, he may be able to contest it in court, saying, "*Hey, I was handed this two days before my marriage. What was I expected to do; not sign it?*" A scenario such as this could cause the prenup to be invalid. Some states don't require a witness to your signatures, but in my opinion, it is always wise to have a witness sign. That way, you have someone else who can testify in case something goes wrong.

If you feel you are unable to discuss a prenuptial with your partner, that speaks to a communication problem; which you need to solve before taking your vows. Ask yourself if you're afraid this person is going to think differently about you or be angry with you. If this is the case, you are better off knowing ahead of time whether your partner is getting into this marriage because of the relationship or because of the money.

ARE YOU COVERED?

Another item to consider is homeowner's insurance. If you are moving into your partner's home, make sure their insurance also covers your belongings. You may come to the marriage with a lot of jewelry, and you may want to consider updating the homeowner's policy to include your valuables. If you have a coin collection, paintings, or anything of significant value, make sure the policy is up-to-date to cover those items as well.

Another important issue is long-term care insurance. If you are getting married again, chances are you are not entering a young marriage, but you are probably in good health. Consider buying some type of insurance that will protect you in case your spouse gets sick. Determine if either of you have enough money so that the respective spouse does not have to exhaust their funds on nursing care. If you are entering into marriage, remember you must be prepared to take the good with the bad, so do your best to plan for the worst.

Think carefully before you make the decision to put your new spouse on the deed of a home you own or on a joint bank account because as soon as you place your "new spouse" on your asset, it automatically becomes marital. Even if you come to the marriage with a $1 million account, if you make it a joint account at that time, then the full million automatically becomes a marital asset because you are giving up your individual asset.

One of my clients was totally convinced that she found the man of her dreams and that she was going to live happily ever after, so she went ahead and put her new husband's name on everything. Nine years later, when they divorced, everything became a marital asset, and it all had to be divided. She came to the marriage with $300,000, and it grew to $500,000. The whole $500,000 was considered a marital asset, and she got $250,000 in the settlement. Had she kept her assets just in her name, they would have been protected and the $300,000 would have remained hers as well as the additional $100,000 from splitting the growth.

I do understand why women make poor decisions. They say to me, "*I don't want to hurt his feelings. I don't want him to think that I don't love him.*" But the sad reality is that we simply cannot know how things are going to go. You may love your partner, and everything could be great for nine years, but things can eventually fall apart.

Do not make decisions based on feelings. You must put your emotions aside. This has nothing to do with your love; this has nothing to do with how you feel about each other. This has everything to do with finances; you need to have safeguards in place for everyone's protection. If your fiancé doesn't like the idea of you protecting your assets, ask yourself why. There are too many examples of people who marry for what they think is love, only to discover that the other party married for money. Don't be duped.

Last, if you are merging your households, consider talking with your children about things they may want you to keep for them. Often, children have sentimental attachments to items we do not know about, so be as open as you can with your children. Develop and foster transparency in order to facilitate an easier transition into the new marriage and to build a stronger foundation for your newly formed family.

Action Checklist

Chapter Five: Love and Remarriage

- ☐ Make a list of each individual's assets and debts.

- ☐ Discuss how your assets will be disbursed upon death.

- ☐ Seek the assistance of an attorney in drafting a prenuptial agreement.

- ☐ Be upfront, honest, and transparent.

- ☐ Decide if you need long-term care insurance to protect your assets.

- ☐ Know your state laws regarding asset protection, distribution and division.

Chapter Six

CHANGING JOBS /
BACK TO WORK

Changing jobs, going back to work, or becoming self-employed can be stressful and rewarding at the same time. There are important decisions you should consider during such transitions that will impact your financial picture. In this chapter, we explore these decisions and focus on ways for you to save for your retirement.

Let's first consider a job change. If you have a 401(k) plan at your current place of employment and you have been hired at a new company that offers a 401(k) plan, you should consider transferring your plan to your new place of employment. It is best to contact the new company plan administrator to determine if this is possible. While you may be permitted to leave your 401(k) investment with the prior company or roll it over into an IRA, I usually recommend that you consolidate your investments under fewer roofs. Over many years, I have seen clients frequently leave their retirement plans at their prior places of employment. Over their lifetime with each successive job change, there are subsequently several retirement plans held at multiple companies. When I work with widows who have recently lost their spouse, one of the first questions I ask is *"Did your spouse have any 401(k) plans at their place of employment?"* Unfortunately, I typically get a puzzled response. Trying to locate a loved one's assets can be daunting. If your spouse had a small retirement account or pension plan with a prior employer, the company or union will not be reaching out to you upon their death. If your spouse did not maintain correspondence with the prior plan administrators, you may not be able to receive account information. Perhaps you've moved, and your old address on record is no longer forwarded. If the plan administrator cannot reach you, your money gets designated as an unclaimed asset. This is one of the primary reasons that I am a strong believer in consolidating retirement accounts.

Although I advocate merging 401(k) plans together, I certainly would not encourage you to move the assets into the new employer's plan if it does not suit your needs. Remember, you can roll your 401(k) into an IRA. IRAs offer a wide variety of investment options compared to 401(k)s, which are typically confined to the plan offerings. However, 401(k)s have an advantage; account owners can take loans against them if they are strapped for funds. While I don't advise it, this may be the only viable alternative for some. IRAs do not offer a loan provision, and moving funds out of an IRA prematurely is cost prohibitive. At this point, you might be thinking, *"I already have an IRA rollover with my investment advisor; I don't want to have all my eggs in one basket. Maybe I should keep my 401(k) plan where it is even though I am leaving the firm or retiring."* This may appeal to investors who think that this is a way to diversify their holdings. The important note here is to realize that consolidating investments under one advisor is not the same as having all your eggs in the same basket. When financial strategists advise investors to diversify their holdings, they are recommending a balanced portfolio allocation, not a scattering of investments at multiple advisory firms or placement of investments under multiple plan administrators.

Having serviced clients for nearly thirty years, I have witnessed an array of investor inclinations. Some of my seasoned clients, for example, have benefited from company stock options for years. While it is all well and good to hold some company stock, I advise them to diversify and purchase mutual funds as well. Take inventory of stock options frequently, especially when retiring or transitioning to another job.

It is not unusual for widows to hold onto their loved one's company stocks for a prolonged time. Case in point, my father worked for IBM for over thirty years and built up a pretty impressive holding of IBM shares. My mother had a difficult time letting go of his IBM stock; when dad passed away, mom was emotionally attached to the holdings. She couldn't be talked into diversifying her investment; on some level, she felt that she would be betraying my father. I see this type of rationale with my clients as well. Some of them have emotional ties to their company stock holdings and simply refuse to sell or diversify. I have also found that a fair amount of these clients believe that their stocks are secure because they think these large companies will be around forever. I am sure that the majority of the people who worked for WorldCom, Enron, Digital Equipment, or American Airlines never thought that those companies would be in the kind of financial trouble that forced them into bankruptcy, reorganization, or corporate takeover.

The message here is that you want to make sure you are not overly invested in one particular company. If that firm fails and goes into bankruptcy or falls on hard times, your retirement account is at risk. It is imperative that you have knowledge of your 401(k) holdings and that you have determined that those holdings are appropriate for your needs. For those employed by a firm with a defined-benefit plan (pension), it is important to know your options at retirement. Typically, you can receive a lump-sum payment or an annuitized distribution. Just remember, if the company is sold, the new company may decide to discontinue the plan. You will get some type of payout under such a scenario, but it may likely be less than what you anticipated at retirement.

KNOW YOUR PENSION PLAN OPTIONS

If you are employed and have a pension plan, you should consider what happens if or when you leave the company or retire. I recommend that you speak with the plan administrator to understand your plan's options well before you make the transition. Some pension plans offer a lump-sum distribution at the time you retire. In this case, you simply get a cash distribution. Alternatively, you can choose to get income for the rest of your life, either jointly or singly. The single-life payout is based solely on you, the employee. The joint-life payout is based on you and your spouse. The joint-life payout is lower than the single-life option. Prior to making a decision in this regard, it is advisable that you and your spouse review your budget and retirement plans. Your spouse may want a say in the matter. It is important to consider your surviving spouse's income stream if you select a single-life option. Under the single-life payout, the income stream stops upon the participant's death. With the joint-life selection, despite a lower payout, your spouse will continue to receive payments if you die for the remainder of her life.

When I prepare a financial plan that involves a pension, it is important to analyze the cash flow. If my clients opt to take the single-life payout schedule, I recommend they purchase a term-life policy on the pension owner in case he/she dies first. The difference between the single versus joint-life monthly payout can be used to purchase life insurance. Far too often I have witnessed couples purchase a supplemental life policy, and then after about ten or fifteen years into retirement, they decide to discontinue the policy due to premium increases. Unfortunately, in some cases soon after terminating the policy, the participant dies, and the surviving wife is left without the life insurance policy or the pension.

While we are hardwired to think our end of life is well in the future, we must plan as if it isn't. We need to consider multiple scenarios, making sure that we are making the best decision for both parties in the relationship. In some circumstances, I have counseled clients to take a lump-sum distribution rather than the pension plan, particularly when the integrity of the company is at stake. It is wise to properly evaluate the company's bottom line to gauge its longevity. There is no need to put your pension plan at risk if the company isn't going to survive; even in cases where the company can restructure, your pension payment could be severely lowered. In tenuous situations like this, it is frequently best to take the lump-sum payment if available. It is also advisable to take a lump sum payment if the plan is underfunded. Remember there is no guarantee that you will receive your full pension payments if the company or plan is on shaky ground. Taking a distribution gives you the opportunity to roll over the funds into an IRA and invest the money independently. While it's not a guarantee, you can probably invest in a way that, over time, will average a 6 percent annual return. Assessing your risks and maximizing your gains is an important part of this process. I periodically discuss these issues with my clients. It is recommended that you have a conversation with your advisor about your pension fund options.

DEALING WITH WINDFALLS

Company bonuses are rewarding and attractive; however, you need to be aware of tax implications. In an effort to minimize the tax consequence, it is best to evaluate the offering with your accountant. Key corporate executives may be offered a nonqualified plan. This is a tax-deferred retirement plan that is not required to follow the Employee Retirement Income Security Act (ERISA) guidelines. Typically, distributions from these plans are made over a set period of time. It is important to know that the deferred compensation in a nonqualified plan must remain unsecured, which makes the funds available to the employer's creditors. When you retire, the assets are typically distributed according to an arranged payment plan. Other plans may require an immediate payout, so it is critical to know your choices. Although nonqualified plans allow you to defer taxes on your income into the future, it is necessary to weigh the pros and cons of such a plan. As a key executive, the company may require you to participate in this type of plan to tie you to the company. You have become an integral part of how that company moves forward; you are basically tied in with your investment.

One of my clients was recently confronted with this situation. As she moved up the ranks in her company, she had to contribute to the company's nonqualified plan, which meant that she became tied to the firm. She was told that upon her retirement she would take distributions over ten years. I asked her, "*Why aren't you maximizing your contribution to your 401(k)? You should be doing that before you defer money to the nonqualified plan.*" The rude reality is the company no longer allowed her to make contributions to her qualified plan. Planning for her future is difficult. Should the company fall on hard times, the nonqualified plan may evaporate. The amount she has in the plan is considerable and will continue to grow over her next ten years of employment. The primary issue is that her retirement is "hinging" on her receiving the payments. It is unfortunate she has all her eggs in one basket. We discussed other possibilities for securing her future. Our plan is to put aside after-tax money in an investment account every year. This is why I strongly suggest that you know exactly what you are getting into when you start a new job. Your compensation package is important and could involve some risk.

Upon exiting a company, you may get a "golden parachute" or a severance package, and you need to know how it will be paid and what it entails. Is it tied to company stock? Is it a lump-sum payment or is it paid out over time?

To be considered a "parachute payment" the benefits need to fall under section 280G of the Internal Revenue Code. Most packages (contracts) are an established agreed upon compensation that top-level executives will receive upon termination. These incentives play a part in all types of corporate business. The golden parachute still exists today, and there is much controversy surrounding the practice.

Severance packages are not regarded as a parachute payment. Typically, a severance package is based upon years of service. The severance agreement will usually include terms of payment, COBRA information, a non-compete clause, general release of claims, unemployment information, covenant not to sue, and your retirement plan information if applicable. It is important to consider other compensation you may be owed. If you have stock options, are they accelerated? Does your company owe you for unreimbursed business expenses? If your pay is commission or bonus based, are you owed further compensation? It may be beneficial to defer a portion of the severance into the next tax year when possible. This requires some planning; in cases where you are dealing with a small company, there may be some flexibility and consideration for your concerns. Most large companies, however, offer a one-time payment.

KNOW YOUR COMPENSATION PACKAGE

Before accepting a new position, ask yourself *Is this what I want? Is this what I'm looking for?* It can appear great on paper, but is the job right for you? Are the benefits meeting your needs? Some people accept a new position based on salary and are less concerned about the benefits. Often, people, especially those new to the workforce, do not fully understand their compensation package—particularly their 401(k) plans. They come out of their employee orientation with a fairly large amount of paperwork. They need time to review the material but frequently do not and consequently miss enrollment deadlines.

Sign up for the 401(k) plan as soon as you are able. Look at your budget, determine how much you can afford to set aside, and commit to it. When I am working with my younger clients just out of school, I suggest that they start putting aside 7–10 percent of their income into their retirement account. I understand this is a paltry rate, but I also understand that this age demographic tends to spend more. They have an active social life, they have student loans, they need to build a work wardrobe, and I don't want them to run into credit card debt for such things. But, for my older clients who are either re-entering the workforce or changing jobs, I encourage them to maximize their contributions. What they do not receive, they do not spend.

Evaluate the firm's life and disability insurance offerings. Life and disability insurance are an important consideration in contingency planning. If you were to die or become disabled, do you have adequate insurance? You need to give careful thought as to what your family's needs would be should a catastrophic event occur. A firm's group plan usually costs less than private plans on the market. Most companies provide standard disability, but have you determined if you might need additional private coverage? What if you are eventually unable to perform your occupation, how much is that going to cost? Knowing the specifics about the disability plans available to you could spare you unpleasant surprises down the road. Consider a situation that could result in you being partially disabled. Would your disability coverage require you to work a menial job, disqualifying you from benefits?

Many people feel awkward evaluating these types of scenarios. It is human nature to avoid these considerations. But as an employee and head of household, you should know your options and consider a multitude of possibilities.

So, you just joined a new company with benefits. Is the health coverage adequate? If you take the coverage, how much will it cost you? This is not a simple matter. What types of health care packages are there? Do you want the PPO (preferred provider organization), the HMO (health maintenance organization), the POS (point of service plan), or an indemnity plan? Do you want a high deductible or a low deductible plan, with or without co-insurance?

What is best for your needs? Obviously, you must first make sure you can afford the plan. Are you offered dental and vision insurance? If you are unsure, ask your company's HR representative. Be sure to evaluate all offerings and consider all your needs.

HOW DO I MANAGE MY 401(K)S?

In my line of business, I find that many of my clients manage their 401(k) accounts in a couple of different ways. One client transfers her money from her old 401(k) and consolidates it into her new 401(k) plan every time she changes her job. She is comforted knowing her retirement funds are in one place. On the other hand, I have clients with retirement accounts in multiple places. One client expressed her difficulty in managing four different plans. She thought she needed to wait until she was age fifty-nine and a half to consolidate them. I explained that she could roll them over into an IRA once she separated from the company. She then asked, "Well, then how can I invest my funds?" I told her she could invest it in whatever she liked (individual stocks, mutual funds, etc.). She was enlightened by this news and no longer felt trapped in the multiple plans.

If you get a pay raise, remember that you will likely owe more taxes on that extra income. It is wise to budget your increased wage. Consider maximizing your 401(k) contribution, if you have not reached the limit, which will help lower your tax obligation. Pay yourself before you pay the government. Let's say, for instance, you were making $90,000, and you receive a raise to $125,000 a year. Use that extra income to maximize your 401(k) contributions. If you are already maximizing your contribution, look at other investment options. Depending on your total income, you may be able to make a Roth IRA contribution, and although it has no immediate tax savings, it can provide tax-free growth over its lifetime. Also, if your employer offers a Roth 401(k), speak with your advisor—it may make sense to elect nondeductible contributions. If your company offers a match, it must flow into the tax-deferred portion of the 401(k) while a smaller amount of your contribution can fund a tax-free Roth 401(k). This could be advantageous from a tax perspective. Do the tax calculations, and consider the results. Your analysis may demonstrate that electing to fund the Roth provides you with tax-free dollars in the future, which outweigh the tax savings today.

ARE YOU A 1099 WORKER?

"Self-employed" does not mean, "not paying taxes." I have a client who recently changed from a W-2 salaried employee to a 1099 independent contractor. She called saying, *"Now that I am working for myself, I have so much more money since I don't have to pay taxes. It's really great having all of this extra cash."* I answered back saying, *"Hold it—you can't be spending that money. You still owe Uncle Sam."* I advised my client to notify her accountant that she is no longer salaried but contracted. If you get Misc-1099 income, you need to be putting money aside to pay quarterly estimated taxes. Sometimes newly self-employed people think that they continue to pay taxes once a year; this is not the case when you're self-employed, if you do not make estimated quarterly estimated payments, you are hit with a failure to pay penalty, as well as interest charges on the amount that was due. Furthermore, you will have to manage a large tax bill at the end of the year.

Individuals who become self-employed should consider a retirement savings plan. If you are paid via a 1099, you can open a SEP IRA and put away 20 percent of your net income (up to the maximum specified by the IRS). If you are the sole proprietor and the only employee, you can open what's called a My-K or an individual 401(k). It is so important to open an account and to start saving as soon as possible for your future. As mentioned, you can also consider setting up a Roth 401(k) plan that will provide you with tax-free growth as well as funds that can be withdrawn in retirement that are nontaxable. There are plenty of options out there—it is a matter of looking at what you earn and which savings plan will give you the greatest benefit.

Since we are discussing the advantages of investing in a Roth, let's back up and answer the question, "*What is a Roth IRA or Roth 401(k)?*" A Roth plan allows you to invest after-tax dollars in a retirement account. While there are no tax benefits today, the Roth does provide a tax-free investment vehicle for your future. The key point here is that monies will not be taxed when withdrawn. Think of this savings vehicle as an umbrella. Under the Roth umbrella, you have the Roth IRA and the Roth 401(k) plan. This umbrella allows only "after-tax dollars" into the plans, but all growth is tax-free. These accounts will provide you with a tax-free withdrawal bucket in retirement.

And here's a bonus tip for parents of teens or young adults who are still dependents: if your child is employed, you may want to encourage them to open a Roth IRA. If your child is a minor, open one up on his or her behalf. I tell my clients that this is the best investment for any child who is working because they typically do not earn enough to pay taxes. It is essentially tax-free money going into a tax-free investment vehicle. It is a layup. If your child spent the money he or she made from their employment, and you have the means to make the contribution for them, you should. Most people do not take advantage of this offering. My son has been working since the age of fifteen, and every year, I make the contribution to his custodial Roth IRA, helping him build a little nest egg, and when he's fifty-nine and a half years old, he'll thank me for it!

Action Checklist

Chapter Six: Changing Jobs / Back to Work

- ☐ Carefully review the company's compensation package before taking a job.

- ☐ Understand your benefits package fully and sign up right away for retirement plans that are available to you.

- ☐ Find out what savings vehicles your company offers.

- ☐ Consolidate your retirement plans.

- ☐ Take advantage of Roth plans.

- ☐ Make Roth contributions for working children.

Chapter Seven

READY FOR RETIREMENT?

How do you ensure that your retirement is as comfortable and stress-free as possible? You need to determine what will create the best income stream and then you will need to manage it appropriately.

Many people think once they retire, they should shift more of their assets into a fixed-income investment, forgetting that they need to keep their money growing. Conventional thought dictated that you increase your fixed-income holdings according to your age. This led many people to shift their money out of the equity market and into bonds when they retired. Today, however, retirees should consider that they might be living longer in retirement. As a result, their money needs to continue to grow, not sit gathering minimal interest. Some retirees consider buying a fixed annuity so they can have an income stream. Having an income stream is important, and the annuity can create that for you. However, you need to be aware of how you set up your annuity payment election. Much like a company pension, once you annuitize the policy, the money is no longer yours. So, what happens if you are two years into an annuity and you die? Similar to the company pension, it depends on the elections you made. Did you opt for the single-life, joint-life, or period-certain payment? Understanding your elections can help to prevent an unwelcome surprise.

The more features you attach to an annuity, the greater impact it will have on internal fees or a payment stream. For example, if you select a payout based upon both you and your spouse's lifetime vs. your lifetime only, the income flow may be reduced (depending on the circumstances), because chances are one of you is going to outlive the other. It is important to make sure you fully understand the annuity options before making an investment as these products are contracts and generally cannot be changed.

WILL YOUR INVESTMENTS COVER YOUR NEEDS?

Instead of cashing in on your investments, you should be asking *"What can I withdraw from these investments to meet my objectives?"*

The first priority is to build a budget. What is your income stream? What are your expenses? This establishes your base. Now ask yourself, do you want to travel? How often do you want to buy a car? Is the house paid off? Do you have any loans, if so, how many and for how much? Is your spouse still working? Are both of you retired, with two sources of Social Security income? Once you know what you have and what you need, you can assess your base. If your expenses are nearly in line with your income, with a small negative gap remaining, calculate what your investments can pay out to potentially fill the gap. Your plan should extend at least twenty to thirty years out, depending on when you retire. If you do not have a plan; it is time to get one.

If you cannot create your own financial plan, hire a Certified Financial Planner (CFP) to create one for you. Be leery of advisors and brokers who call themselves "professional" financial planners, they may not have the credentials, training or ethical obligation to represent your best interest.

Typically retired clients depend on monthly distributions from their investment accounts to supplement their cash flow. The ideal approach to investing is a blended portfolio between fixed income and equities to match your risk tolerance. This will enable you to remain invested during volatile markets. The objective is to design a portfolio to produce good, reliable returns over a long period of time to meet your retirement goals. Once you have established the appropriate allocation that matches your risk tolerance, it is important to rebalance your portfolio periodically.

When you look at the current makeup of your investments, ask yourself "*Are my investments well positioned for my future?*" Important factors include the expected rate of return on investments, the inflation rate, and your tax rate; equally important are your future personal expenditures. These factors are used to determine the real rate of return. For example, if your investments are earning 5 percent but inflation is running at 3 percent, then your real return is only 2 percent. Also, remember that if your taxes are increasing, you may want your investments growing in a qualified tax-deferred account rather than a nonqualified taxable account.

Typically, retirees are advised to withdraw from their taxable investments first and save their tax-deferred instruments for last. The reasoning stems from tax-deferred accounts that provided higher growth since they are sheltered from taxes. However, I don't believe in that methodology. I think retirees should always have different investment vehicles at their disposal. For example, I encourage people to have a Roth IRA because it is able to grow and be distributed tax-free There are times when it makes sense to withdraw from a rollover IRA account. There are other times when it is more beneficial to withdraw from a Roth IRA. Yet, there are situations when taking from a brokerage account is most desirable. Maintaining different investment vehicles gives you choices and can lead to maximizing your income stream in retirement.

HOW DOES YOUR STATE TAXES COMPARE TO OTHER STATES?

State taxes are a major consideration that should be part of your retirement planning. To fully understand the effect of taxes, let's evaluate the following: Assume you are currently in the 15 percent federal tax bracket and have an additional 5.3 percent state tax obligation. This means that if you want to net, after taxes, $70,000 from your IRA, you will need to withdraw $87,829.36 to account for tax payments. That is an additional $17,829.36 needed to pay the 15 percent federal tax and 5.3 percent state tax. Taxes erode an IRA if there is a constant need for large distributions. I strongly recommend that people, who are on the verge of retirement, living in high-tax states consider moving to a lower-tax state to increase their distribution flow from retirement funds.

If you have multiple investment account types that provide you a source of income, it may not be as arduous a task to get funds as it would if you only have a   tax-deferred investment account. For a better understanding of the tax ramifications, let's look at an example.

Consider the previous example of a net distribution of $70,000, with a 15 percent federal income tax withholding and a 5.3 percent state income tax withholding. The following chart shows the tax effect of withdrawing money from various savings vehicles and why it is important to have options.

Distribution Amount from IRA Assets	Distribution Amount from Roth IRA Assets	Distribution Amount from Investment Assets	Gross	Taxes
$70,000	$0	$0	$87,829.36	$17,829.36
$35,000	$35,000	$0	$78,914.68	$8,914.68
$25,000	$22,500	$22,500	$76,367.63	$6,367.63

In the first distribution, the full $70,000 comes out of the IRA and has a tax consequence of $17,829.36. If you happen to have an IRA and a Roth IRA, you could take a portion from each (as shown in the second distribution). Here, the tax is considerably less since the Roth is a tax-free instrument. Lastly, if you have an IRA, Roth IRA, and a taxable investment account, and you took a portion from each, the tax ramification is reduced to $6,367.63. Having multiple investment buckets helps you avoid eroding your principal to pay for taxes.

I recommend that people consider their state's tax rates when they are planning where they want to retire. Newly retired clients of mine recently sold their house in Sudbury, Massachusetts, and moved to Florida. They chose Florida because they do not want to see their savings eaten up by taxes. When they start taking money from their IRAs during retirement, that money will have a federal tax obligation but not a state obligation because Florida does not levy state taxes. Every little bit helps. On the $70,000 net distribution from the IRA I was discussing previously, the tax you would pay if you live in Florida would be $12,352.94, versus $17,829.36, since you eliminated the 5.3 percent state income tax. Thus, you will save approximately $5,476.42.

If you can manage a move and can buy a less expensive home in Florida, why wouldn't you? The couple from Sudbury could pocket

$300,000 from the sale of their Massachusetts home, which they can put into an investment account that will grow and can be used to fund their long-term care needs. Depending on age, you may find that you have no need or desire for a house. You might be better served living in a condo that is maintenance-free.

If you saved enough to meet your goals, without having to move, then you are well on your way to a stress-free retirement - congratulations! However, if your needs are not being met, I recommend you consider relocation in retirement. There are a lot of people who don't move because they want to stay close to family and friends. Their strong social network is important to them, and this is a reasonable consideration. Many of my clients have children, grandchildren, and/or a social network where they live, and because this is what is important to them, they choose not to move.

QUESTIONS TO CONSIDER BEFORE MOVING:

- What is your reason for moving?
- Do you need the money from the sale of your home?
- What is the cost of living where you currently live versus where you would relocate?
- Do you know anyone where you are considering moving?
- What is important to you about your current community?

Drafting a pros/cons list is helpful in making any decision. What are you gaining vs. losing if you move? At first, just brainstorm, then go back and prioritize what is most important on the list.

Do you have a mortgage? You don't want to be paying on a mortgage when you are eighty years old, but if you take out a thirty-year mortgage when you are fifty-five, you will be doing just that.

Consider either downsizing your housing in terms of price, size, or both or alternatively, refinance your mortgage to a fifteen-year term if you can afford it. I advise my clients to go into retirement with little debt, which is why I recommend avoiding car loans. There are so many people who have never learned how to handle money and retirement isn't the time to be hanging onto those bad habits.

HAVE YOU CONSIDERED LONG-TERM CARE?

Long term care is an important consideration in retirement. If you do not have long-term care insurance and you are in good health, I suggest you look at policies. If you are in your sixties and there are no red flags, take time to evaluate the plan and assess its value given your family health history, support network, and other late-life considerations.

If you're married and considering long-term care coverage, find a policy that is transferable between husband and wife. One of my married clients recently purchased a plan that is transferable; their premium is around $4,500 per year, and it covers a total of six years of long-term care. This means that if one of them enters a nursing home for a year, the policy will still cover the healthy spouse when and if needed. I believe it is important to have a feature similar to this, as typically, the husband stays at home because the wife is able to care for him, so if he goes into a nursing home, it is generally for a shorter period of time. Upon his death, his wife has the remaining benefit, as she may enter a nursing home for a longer period of time since there is no one to care for her. The average stay in a nursing home is three years, so you need to plan accordingly. Long-term plans change all the time, so make sure you get the most up-to-date information available and do shop around.

You want to make sure your policy is backed by a strong insurance company; choose a double-A-rated or triple-A-rated firm. Most contracts have add-ons or riders. When you are looking at riders, consider an inflation-adjustment rider. This will allow the daily benefit to keep up with inflation. Also offered is a feature called the elimination period. This is the period of time in which you self-fund your care before the policy kicks in. A ninety-day elimination period is usually standard. Typically, a longer elimination period will lower the premium.

Once you have a long-term care policy, you need to determine how much you'll need to supplement your long-term care. If the policy is paying for half of your stay or three-quarters of your stay, can you afford to pay the balance? You need to look at your asset pool to make that determination. You want to buy a policy that fits within the scope of what you have and what you need; do not just buy whichever policy you're sold. By doing some homework, you can evaluate what coverage you can afford, along with any additional riders that are important to you.

Another component you want to consider in a long-term care policy is whether or not you are covered for at-home care. If your policy pays out $300 per day, it should be $300 a day regardless if you are at home or in a nursing home facility. You should also be sure to check that once the policy becomes active, your premium stops. Most of these riders are standard in the policy, so you are not asking for something that is out of the ordinary.

Rather than purchasing long-term care insurance, some people prefer to put money aside on a regular basis and invest it in an account they could tap to cover long-term care if/when needed. This is a good strategy if you are disciplined. If your premiums are cost prohibitive, creating a bucket specifically for health care is another way to safeguard your future. However, be aware that the high cost of nursing-home services can quickly deplete funds you have set aside for care, which may not last as long as needed.

Keep in mind that the cost of nursing homes is dependent on location. If you move to the southern part of the country, you'll find very nice nursing homes that cost significantly less than they do in the Northeast. The parents of a colleague of mine lived in New England. When the parents could no longer care for themselves, the children sold their parent's home, moved them to South Carolina, and put them in a beautiful facility at half of what it would have cost in New England. They were fortunate to have family in South Carolina, so the move was easy. If your assets are not going to give you the amount or the quality of care that you desire, you need to get creative and stay open-minded about the future. It can be a difficult choice to relocate, particularly if it means you'll be far from family, home and community.

OTHER THINGS TO CONSIDER AS YOU ENTER RETIREMENT:

If you have trusts or wills, you should review them every five to ten years to make sure that they are still in order because things change. For example, you may have created the trust when you had minor children, who are now adults with children of their own. In retirement, your schedule should allow you time to meet with your attorney to get things in order. You should want to know that your wishes are all set. Make sure you have a health care proxy and a power of attorney in place as well.

Often, people make the mistake of setting up a trust and never funding it. When one of my business associates passed away unexpectedly, his wife told me, "We set up a trust for the kids to get $100,000 each." The husband had three children from a prior marriage. The trust was created to ensure his children were to inherit a portion of his wealth. When the husband passed, his wife got all the money. How did that happen? The husband created a trust and a trust account, but he had never funded the account. This can be corrected, but it takes time, effort and money to get it right. Remember, if you are going to go through the trouble and cost of setting up a trust, make sure that it is properly funded.

Ideally, retirement is when we get to enjoy the fruits of our hard work. If you are prepared, then enjoy yourself! If you are still preparing, don't ignore it or somehow imagine that things will take care of themselves. They almost never do, and a lottery ticket is not a viable retirement strategy.

Action Checklist

Chapter Seven: Ready for Retirement

- ☐ Review and make adjustments to your asset allocation in retirement if necessary.

- ☐ Look at your current investments, should you consider any changes?

- ☐ Build a retirement plan—Consult with a Certified Financial Planner (CFP®).

- ☐ Know your tax situation particularly at the state level.

- ☐ Do plan for your long-term care; consider buying insurance or set-up a funding strategy.

- ☐ Review legal documents for life-event changes that may have taken place over the years.

- ☐ If you have a trust, make sure it is funded.

.

Chapter Eight

SOCIAL SECURITY/ MEDICARE—WHAT IS YOUR BEST STRATEGY?

As a financial advisor, I am often asked, *"When should I apply for Social Security?"* There is no single right answer to this question because when you take it depends on your needs. Ideally, you should wait at least until full retirement age in order to get your full benefit. There are situations that may cause you to apply for benefits before full retirement age. If, for example, you are laid off from work, or you are unable to get a job, and you are not at your full retirement age but are at least sixty-two years old, you may have to apply for early benefits. If you need income and you do not have enough savings, tapping into your Social Security benefits early (at a reduced rate) may be your only option. Is this the best option? No, but if you have no other choice, it certainly has its merits.

On the flipside, if you are working, if you have income, and if you don't need to take your Social Security benefit, then your best choice is to wait as long as you possibly can before collecting. If you are still working at age sixty-seven (your full-retirement age) and you do not plan to retire soon, then delaying your benefit will allow it to grow at a rate of 8 percent per year until you reach the age of seventy. At seventy years old, all benefits stop increasing, so there is no reason to wait any longer to file. If you were born between 1943 and 1954, your full retirement age is sixty-six. For those born after 1954, full-retirement age increases by two months each year thereafter. So, if you were born in 1955, full retirement age is sixty-six and two months, and if you were born in 1956, full-retirement age is age sixty-six and four months, and so on. This continues until 1960, where full-retirement age is currently set at age sixty-seven.

YEAR OF BIRTH	FULL RETIREMENT AGE
1943-1954	66
1955	66 and 2 months
1956	66 and 4 months
1957	66 and 6 months
1958	66 and 8 months
1959	66 and 10 months
1960 or later	67

Originally, full-retirement age was set at sixty-five for everyone; however, in 1983, Congress mandated the change to strengthen Social Security finances.

Many clients have requested my consultation regarding their optimal time to request benefits. Do they take benefits at their full retirement age, do they begin at age sixty-two, or do they wait until they are seventy to get full maximization? The best way to determine the optimal time to take benefits is to establish the break-even point. The breakeven point is determined when the amount of your Social Security (at full retirement age) is equal to the amount received for waiting to maximize the benefit. Typically, the break-even point is somewhere between fourteen and sixteen years. For example, if your full retirement age is sixty-five, and you began receiving your Social Security benefit at age sixty-five instead of waiting the extra five years to get the maximum benefit, you would break even somewhere around age eighty. So why wait? This is a crucial question. An important consideration is your family genetics; is there a pattern of longevity? If your parents lived into their eighties or nineties or hundreds, then you have a greater chance to maximize your Social Security benefits because you are likely to live beyond the break-even point. If you have enough assets to live comfortably until age seventy and your family line tends to be long-lived, then you should consider waiting until you are seventy to file.

When Social Security was created, actuarial data showed that most individuals did not live past age sixty-five. Thanks to modern medicine that has changed; people are typically living into their eighties and nineties. Given the demands on Social Security, whether it is going to "be there" indefinitely is a topic beyond the scope of this book, but it is certainly fair to say that it was never planned to serve as many people as it does now. The viability of the program is frequently a discussion in political arenas.

To summarize, you have three options for taking your Social Security benefits: (1) you can take it early and accept a reduced benefit, (2) you can wait until your designated full retirement age and get your full benefits, or (3) you can wait to collect until you are age seventy and get the largest possible benefit to maximize your monthly income.

HOW ARE BENEFITS CALCULATED?

Social Security is based on your lifetime earnings. The Social Security Administration calculates your average indexed monthly earnings over the thirty-five years in which you have earned the most money—not necessarily the most recent or consecutive years but your highest earning years. They apply a formula to calculate your benefit—often called your primary insurance amount (PIA). This is the indexed return based on actual earnings that are adjusted to account for changes in your average wages since the year you started earning money.

If you want to know your benefit, login to the Social Security website (www.ssa.gov) and use their "benefit calculator." You will be asked to enter your Social Security number, date of birth, and some other information before you are provided with the range of potential benefit amounts available to you at different filing ages. The calculator offers only an estimate because your future wages are not known. A word of caution: Make sure the Social Security website you access is the official government site! Do not be fooled into putting your sensitive, personal information on a lookalike site. Although the government prefers that you do everything online, including filing for benefits, I do not recommend that to my clients. Make an appointment to see a benefits administrator at your local office. Bring a list of questions with you and make sure you understand everything you are told.

SPECIAL SITUATIONS

If you are a widow, you can claim benefits as early as age sixty. The amount is based on 100 percent of the amount due at your spouse's full retirement age. It is important to note, however, if you take your benefit as early as age sixty, it will be reduced. The amount of the reduction is a fraction of a percent for each month you claim prior to reaching full retirement age. If you delay taking your benefit until you reach your full retirement age, then you will not be subject to a reduction. Most widowed women receive a higher payment by claiming their husband's benefit instead of their own because most men's salaries are higher than women's and Social Security benefits are a based on income levels.

If you are able to collect Social Security based on your work history, you have a couple of options:

- collect your benefit,

- collect the survivor benefit based on the employment of your late spouse.

If your benefit will be larger at age seventy than the survivor benefit at full retirement age, take the survivor benefit first and defer your benefit until later. You can switch to your higher benefit at age seventy. This option is only available at full retirement age. Note, if you are disabled and a widow, you can start to collect your late husband's benefit at age fifty at the reduced rate.

As an example, I have a young widow client who has not yet reached her sixtieth birthday. She was a stay-at-home mom during her marriage, and now she has gone back to her previous career as an accountant. Her husband was a high-powered doctor earning a high six-figure salary. Even though he died a number of years ago, his Social Security benefit may be much higher than hers due to his superior earnings. I advised her to hold off taking his benefit until she is of full retirement age. Even though she can take the benefit earlier at age sixty, the monthly Social Security check will be reduced and she will no longer have the option to defer her benefit until age seventy.

When she reaches full retirement age, we will review her options prior to filing for her benefit.

SPOUSAL BENEFITS FOR DIVORCEES AND REMARRIED WIDOWS

If you are a widow and getting remarried, that won't affect your survivor benefits—as long as you are sixty years or older when you remarry.

If you are not a widow, but, have been divorced, you may be eligible for spousal benefits from your ex, as long as you were married for at least ten years before the divorce. However, you must be at least sixty-two years old and have been divorced for at least two years to claim the benefit. Furthermore, the benefit that you are entitled to receive based on your own work must be less than the benefit you would receive based on your ex-spouse's work.

If you were divorced and remarried, you cannot collect your ex's benefit unless your second marriage ends. In addition, you can receive benefits even if your ex-spouse has not applied, so long as he qualifies for them. You don't need to have his permission or even his Social Security number. If you are applying for benefits through your ex-spouse, you must show both a marriage certificate and a final divorce decree.

Unlike the widow's benefit, you can only receive the higher payment at the time you apply. There is one caveat: if you are divorced, and your ex-spouse dies, you have the same benefits as the widow.

In addition, if you are a widow or a divorcee, you need to make an appointment at a local office to file for benefits. The Social Security Administration will need to see your supporting documentation, so don't forget to bring along all pertinent information.

MEDICARE AND MEDICAID

Medicare comes into play at age sixty-five or earlier if you are disabled. You have a seven-month window to apply for your benefits. The enrollment period starts three months prior to the month you turn sixty-five, it includes the month in which you turn sixty-five and it ends three months after the month you turn sixty-five. If you don't sign up for Medicare Part B when you're first eligible, you'll have to pay a late enrollment penalty for as long as you have Part B. The penalty can only be avoided if you have an acceptable health plan by Medicare's standard. My best advice is to sign up for Medicare during your enrollment period. If you miss this opportunity, you may have to wait to enroll, which will delay coverage. If you decide that you do not want to take the benefit, that's fine, just be certain that your health care passes the Medicare-approved stipulations to avoid the penalty.

As outlined by the Social Security Administration, the Medicare program has four parts:

- **Part A (hospital insurance):** Hospital insurance helps pay for inpatient care in a hospital or skilled nursing facility (following a hospital stay), some home health care and hospice care.

- **Part B (medical insurance):** Medical insurance helps pay for doctors' visits, and outpatient care (such as diagnostic and laboratory services) as well as durable medical equipment and other supplies that hospital insurance does not cover.

- **Part C (Medicare Advantage Plans):** Medicare Advantage Plans combine Part A and Part B, and often Part D as well as additional benefits such as vision, dental, and hearing. Medicare Advantage plans are offered by private companies and approved by Medicare.

- **Part D (prescription drug coverage):** Prescription drug coverage helps pay for medications doctors prescribe for treatment.

Part A is available at no cost if you or your spouse paid Medicare taxes for 40 quarters while working. If you have not paid enough Medicare taxes to receive Part A benefits at no cost, you are able to purchase the benefit once you reach 65 years old. According to the US government, most people who pay for Part A pay the standard premium. However, if your modified, adjusted gross income reported on your tax return from two years prior is above a certain amount, you may pay an income-related monthly adjustment amount (IRMAA). Due to continual changes in premiums, it is best to visit the Social Security Administration's website to view the most recent cost information.

Part B is available to Medicare-eligible recipients who pay monthly premiums, deductibles, and coinsurance. In 2018, the average standard premium of $134 reflected the monthly cost to most recipients. However, some recipients who receive a Social Security benefit that is not large enough to cover the full Part B premium pay a lower monthly premium. Meanwhile, other recipients with a modified adjusted gross income above a certain amount pay higher monthly premiums. As with Part A, an Income Related Monthly

Adjustment Amount (IRMAA) is used to determine the increased cost. In addition to a monthly premium, Medicare Part B recipients are required to meet a yearly deductible. In 2018, the deductible was $183.

Once the Part B deductible is met, Medicare covers 80 percent of Part B approved medical costs while recipients are responsible for 20 percent of the cost. This is referred to as coinsurance.

Part B premiums and deductible amounts can change each year. The Centers for Medicare and Medicaid Services (CMS) typically announce the rate changes around the middle of October or November.

Part C, the Medicare Advantage Plan, is available as an alternative option to those who are eligible for Medicare Part A, and Part B. Recipients usually pay a monthly premium as well as copays and deductibles. These costs vary from company to company. Unlike the Part B coinsurance of 20 percent, Part C copays are typically fixed amounts (e.g., $10 per PCP visit or $40 per specialist visit). Premiums can range from $0 to $200 per month and deductibles can be significantly higher than the Part B deductible. This plan can also be more restrictive than Part A and Part B, requiring referrals and establishing in-network providers. In some states, if you elect to take the Medicare Advantage Plan, it may be difficult to revert to Medicare.

Part D is a prescription drug plan that has monthly premiums, an annual deductible, and coinsurance. The cost for Part D coverage varies depending on a number of variables such as the prescriptions you take, the plan you choose, and the pharmacy you use. As a Medicare beneficiary, you do not automatically get Part D. Drug coverage is optional for Medicare-eligible recipients, however, if you do not sign up for Medicare Part D coverage when you are first eligible, you may have to pay a late-enrollment penalty if you decide to enroll later.

Generally speaking, when you reach full retirement age, and you are still working, you want to apply for Part D coverage, even if you have your own health coverage at work and you are not going to be using it. Remember your work insurance drug coverage needs to be deemed as "creditable coverage" to avoid penalties. My best advice is to just sign up for everything and defer the pieces you don't need. That way, when you need the benefits after you retire, you will avoid the penalty.

When selecting Medicare Part A and Part B, it is important to acquire a Medicare Supplement Insurance policy – also referred to as a Medigap policy. These products are sold by private health insurance companies and help defray the cost that Medicare will not cover such as deductibles, and coinsurance.

Medicaid, unlike Medicare, is available at any age if you are not covered under any other policy and you lack financial means. As discussed earlier, Medicaid is a government-sponsored health insurance program. The program is funded by both the federal and state governments and provides medical services for people with income below a certain level.

Action Checklist

Chapter Eight: Social Security— What is Your Best Strategy?

☐ Before you reach age sixty-five, take time to review and understand your options for Social Security Benefits.

☐ Know your break-even point.

☐ If you are a divorcee married for more than 10 years, don't forget to consider your Social Security spousal benefit.

☐ If you are a widow, know your Social Security survivors benefits.

☐ If you are still working, review the costs and benefits of your healthcare coverage against all Medicare plans.

☐ You have a 7 month window to sign up for your Medicare benefits. The window begins three months prior to and ends three months after the month of your sixty-fifth birthday. Remember to sign up, even if you are still working.

☐ You can decline Medicare coverage and avoid the penalty if you have a health plan that qualifies as credible coverage by Medicare's standard.

Chapter Nine

INVESTING CONSIDERATIONS

RISK VERSUS RETURN

Balancing risk vs. return is an age-old dilemma in the world of investments. When my clients ask me how much risk they should take, I tell them it is a function of their age, risk, tolerance, spending, needs and wants. I encourage my younger clients to carry more risk because aggressive investments have a high growth potential and my younger clients need to start creating their nest egg. I am less concerned about the risk they take because their investment portfolios have time to recover from market losses in the event of a downturn. Clients nearing retirement, on the other hand, typically have saved throughout their working years. Those savings represent part of their cash flow in retirement. I am more concerned about the risk my retirees take because their investment portfolios do not have time to recover from market losses and those clients need to maintain their cash flow to pay their bills.

Let's assume you and your spouse are 65 years old and are newly retired with savings totaling around $1 million. At your first visit, you may ask me: "How much risk should we take?" One of the first recommendations I would make is to complete an Investor Profile Questionnaire (IPQ). It is designed like a quiz. For every question, there is a corresponding number, so your answers get scored. When we add up all your points, the score reveals the level of risk you are willing to accept on a spectrum that ranges from conservative to aggressive. After completing the questionnaire, I typically recommend that we take a step back and ask some important questions.

- What are your living expenses?

- What is your budget?

- What is on your retirement wish list?

- What are your liquid assets?

- What is your income stream?

I compile all the information generated from the questions above and then I start working on your financial plan. The plan helps shed light on the type of return you are going to need in order to meet your objectives. Let's imagine your goals included traveling abroad every year and buying a new car every five years. Let's also consider that your spending (as a new retiree) is greater than the income you are receiving, therefore you are dipping into your savings. Assume, based on the outcome of your IPQ, that your risk tolerance is moderate. Hence, your portfolio would have a 60/40 allocation (60% stocks and 40% fixed income). Assume also that I generate your financial plan, using a 5 percent annualized rate of return. Under this scenario, your financial plan shows that you will run out of money by age seventy-eight. Given today's actuarial tables, it is very likely both you and your spouse would live well into your eighties. In this case, we need to reevaluate your plan to allow for a longer income stream. We can adjust your plan a couple of ways:

- Presume a higher rate of return on your investments.

- Make adjustments to lower your expenses.

If I assume a higher rate of return for your plan, I will need to make your retirement account more aggressive by adding more equities (stocks) to your portfolio. This will expose you to more volatility (risk). You may not be able to "ride out" the ebbs and flows of the market. You may also be uncomfortable taking on more risk. You may say to me "*We don't want seventy percent of our assets in equities*," my response is, "*Okay, then how can we lower your expenses? What are you willing to give up? Can you live with traveling every other year rather than every year and can you buy a new car every six years rather than every five years?* Assuming you agree, I re-run your financial plan with your preferred portfolio allocation of 60/40, at a 5 percent annual rate of return, and with vacations every other year and a new car purchase every six years. Given this new scenario, the plan shows that you do not run out of money until you are ninety-two years old. This is now your new comfort zone. The message here is clear when my clients want to spend more than their risk tolerance is able to support, they need to compromise on their wants and learn to be comfortable with some difficult decisions.

I firmly believe if people understand their risk/return comfort zone, they are going to fare much better in retirement than those who do not. One of my clients recently called, I manage one of her retirement accounts with a sixty-forty portfolio allocation (60 percent equities and 40 percent fixed income). This client also has a 401(k) plan that is one hundred percent invested in an S&P 500 fund.

During our conversation, my client mentioned that her 401(k) plan is outperforming the retirement account I manage. She asked why her retirement account lagged her 401(k) account. I explained that her 401(k) is one hundred percent in equities and that we had agreed her portfolio that I manage would not be 100 percent invested in equities because the portfolio I manage is going to fund her retirement and she is planning to retire two years from now. When I developed her financial plan, it clearly showed that she did not need to take on more risk and it matched her risk tolerance. Since she wanted to be more conservative, we decided on a sixty-forty allocation. When we modeled her portfolio against the indices that paralleled her underlying assets, the benchmark return was 5.95 percent. Meanwhile, her portfolio had a 6.35 percent rate of return. It was important that she understood what was going on with her investments, and to take responsibility for her choices and decisions along the way. When it comes to investing, everyone wants to be riding the wave as it crests, but as soon as the bottom falls out, everyone wants out.

By managing risk in a portfolio, we help people stay focused on their long-term horizon. It is sometimes just a matter of reminding people that everything is fine as long as the markets are going up, but, what happens when another 2008 comes around and the markets go down? What happens if you are in retirement and you lose 30 percent of your assets in the first year? How does a significant market downturn affect the rest of your retirement? These considerations establish the groundwork that we review with our clients. By doing a financial plan, we develop a road map that suits our client's needs. As described above, we build a portfolio based on an individual's risk tolerance and goals. The plan helps the clients understand how their assets are invested and may eliminate unnecessary risk such as investing exclusively in the S&P 500.

Most people are not comfortable with the idea of having a high-risk portfolio. When the media reports downward swings in the S&P 500, Nasdaq or the Dow Jones Industrial Average, investors are frequently caught up in the frenzy. I believe investors should be focused on whether their investments are meeting their end goals. Why be consumed with the S&P 500 and why benchmark your portfolio against it, if your needs are being met with a diversified portfolio that includes less risky investments such as fixed income funds?

An interesting thing happened to one of my windowed clients a few months ago. Upon the completion of her financial plan, I saw that she only needed to meet a 2 percent return to reach her retirement-goal needs. She thought she needed to have much more equity and thus much more risk in her portfolio to reach her goals. When she found out she did not, we agreed on a more moderate mix of investments —there was no need to knock out the lights. Why risk it?

I often emphasize to my clients a very important consequence of a bear market; the more you lose in a downturn, the more money you need to recover your losses. For example, if you have invested $500,000 and lost 20 percent or $100,000 in a downturn, you should not celebrate a 20 percent gain the next year, because you have not recovered your losses. Your portfolio is not back up to $500,000, do the math, you are still short by 4 percent, or $20,000. My best advice is to try to meet expectations, unfortunately, people just don't understand or appreciate the risk they assume when they are motivated by higher earnings.

While I have discussed the appropriate times when less equity may be desirable, there are of course times when too little equity is not favorable. When my clients reach retirement they typically ask, should I be more conservative? Should my portfolio have less equity?" There is an old adage that says by the time you are seventy years old, your fixed income should match your age: in other words, you should have 70 percent of your portfolio in fixed income and 30 percent in equities. That may have made sense at one point in time, but if you are seventy today, chances are you are going to live to ninety, and that 30/70 allocation may not provide you with an adequate income stream for the rest of your years.

It is common for me to hear retirees say, *"Maybe I should just look at getting some type of fixed-income instrument that gives me a 5 percent return. I can live on 5 percent for the rest of my life."* My first response is, *"Well, how do you know how long you will live?"* My next response is *"Have you had a financial plan done to assure you only need a 5 percent return to live out your entire life expectancy?"* Moreover, during inflationary times, a 5 percent fixed-income return is going to be depreciated, and your real rate of return is going to be decreased by the amount of inflation. So you need to factor in the rate of inflation when you are considering your portfolio rate of return. In my example above, the financial plan I created for my client revealed she only needed a 2 percent rate of return, and that plan took inflation into account. Most of my retirees are not so lucky; they need a higher rate of return that is sufficient for their income stream. My advice is to have a diversified portfolio that can give you both ends; some securities to provide an avenue for growth so that your assets accumulate during retirement to keep up with the cost of living and some fixed assets that protect you from market swings. The following chart offers a visual overview of asset allocation levels.

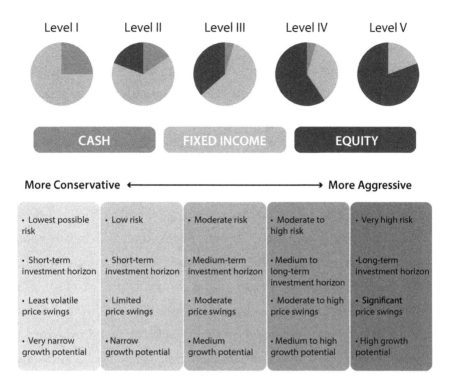

FILL YOUR BUCKETS

Ultimately, the risk vs. return dilemma depends mostly on a point I made earlier, the concept of "buckets." Bucket investing consists of portions of your funds that you divvy up and put to work in different investment vehicles. You may place your funds in something that is going to earn a 5 percent fixed rate of return, that will provide for your income stream. The next portion of funds might be put to work in mostly equities to provide growth to your portfolio. Finally, the remaining bulk of your funds may end up in a well-diversified mutual fund portfolio to supplement your retirement goals.

By doing this, you always have some monies to draw on, and yet you will also have some security in knowing that one portion of what you have is fixed. It is no longer wise (and perhaps never was) to let your age dictate your portfolio allocation.

We are living longer; our life expectancies are increasing every day. That is why it is important to have a long-range plan in place—a real road map that gets you from where you are today to where you will be years from now. Every year, you should revisit your road map and make sure you are still on track. If you are off track, you need to figure out why, then either make changes to rebalance your portfolio or wait it out. Sometimes the market may go up 30 percent followed by a 10 percent drop, then a 20 percent rebound. It is best to look at the average over time and stay focused on the length of your investment period, not the day-to-day swings of the market. That is why financial planning and frequent meetings with your advisor are important. If the portfolio is not on track due to a down year; it does not necessarily mean you should trash the portfolio and start over. It might just mean that you may need to put off buying that new car for an extra year, then when the market recoups, you can buy the car. If you hit a detour, you must regroup and find a way to get back on track. That's what the plan does: it gives you a road map that answers important questions such as *"What's the proper allocation for my investments? Do I have enough assets to meet my needs, and can I retire?"* Even if you have 1 million dollars, when you spend more than what you have, you are going to outlive your money.

One of my clients had a $3 million portfolio, and she was very focused on wanting to retire. But every time we reviewed her plan and her budget, I would tell her that she could not retire because her expenses were too high. She had multiple high-end homes and she was supporting a network of family members. She had backed herself into a corner by creating all these expenses that forced her to keep working to pay the bills. Meanwhile, another client of mine has a portfolio valued at $500,000 and an income from her pension and Social Security that covers her living expenses, so she does not have to draw on her $500,000 worth of assets. This client is able to retire. Why you might ask? Because she lives within her means today and this allows her portfolio to grow for her future cash flow needs.

My number one response to my clients when they ask if they can retire is, "Well, that's up to you. Let's look at your budget, your assets, and your income stream. Let's do an analysis of how you spend money. Are you willing to make adjustments to your spending?" Sometimes, when achieving your goal is on the cusp, we get into the risk/return discussion. If the clients are 3-5 years from retirement, I will talk with them about taking on more risk. More often than not, my clients will reconsider and decide to work another year or two and save a little more money, so they don't have to expose themselves to additional risk. Other times, people are willing to look at their spending and say, "*I can live on a smaller budget. I don't need to go out as often for dinner.*"

WHAT SHOULD BE IN YOUR PORTFOLIO?

When it comes time to invest your savings or reconsider current positions in an existing portfolio, the typical choices are mutual funds, bonds, stocks, and Exchange Traded Funds (ETFs). Is there a right mix? I believe that your portfolio should probably have a little bit of everything. Having a few good blue-chip stocks along with well-performing mutual funds and some fixed income positions is a good balance. Whether you want municipal bonds or corporate bonds and how that mix is going to work depends on your tax bracket. If you are in an upper tax bracket, having municipal bonds should provide you a higher after-tax return because you are earning income that is not being taxed at the federal level versus a corporate bond, which is going to be taxed. In addition, by holding municipal bonds issued by your state of residence, you can avoid state taxes. If you are in a low tax bracket, you may want corporate bonds, which are going to give you a higher yield than municipal bonds.

The investment strategies I use depend heavily on my client's answers to their investment policy statement as mentioned at the beginning of this chapter. Every month I review my client's portfolios, looking at the returns against the benchmark. My first questions are, *Did I meet the benchmark? Did I come close to it? Did I overshoot it?* This is due diligence of a financial advisor as is offering to meet with a client on a regular basis to review the portfolio and their current financial status. It is important to find out if anything has changed in a client's life. I typically ask, "*Did anything change since we last met? Have your views changed? Have your spending habits changed? Has something altered your life that I need to be aware of?*"

I enjoy seeing my clients take proactive measures to meet their most important goals. One of my recently widowed clients was insistent on keeping her family home. When I developed her financial plan, we agreed to a reasonable budget that worked well for her. She goes out a lot less now that her husband is gone, and she is watching her spending. She has consistently kept her budget below the planned amount, and no longer has concerns that she will have to sell her family home; her prudent spending is allowing the portfolio to support her lifestyle and goals. My best advice is to keep your road map current. Track your needs, and your wants, update your financial plan and review your investment policy every three to four years to see if anything has changed.

WHAT SHOULD NEW INVESTORS CONSIDER?

If you are new to investing, make sure the financial advisor you work with has your best interests at heart. I recommend you select an advisor who is a "fiduciary". Fiduciary financial advisors are legally required to act in your best interest. Read the fine print, and be fully aware of the fees that are attached to whatever you buy, these include expense ratios, transaction costs, commissions, and load fees. It is also important to work with an advisor who is experienced in analyzing data, and who is able to offer multiple investment strategies while being aware of potential tax consequences. You don't want someone chasing returns; you want to make sure your advisor uses a sound, methodical approach to investing.

Another very important matter to consider is custodianship. Make sure the investment advisory firm you select does not hold your assets in-house. Your funds should be maintained by a third party custodian such as TD Ameritrade, Fidelity, or Charles Schwab. Third part custodianship is vital to avoid falling into the hands of a firm run by the likes of a Bernie Madoff and other dishonest advisors who access clients' money for personal gains. When your assets are managed by a financial advisor and are held by a custodian, you will receive a separate statement of your account(s) from the custodian. You are able to see exactly what you own from an unbiased third party. A financial advisor should not generate your statements, but rather should provide a quarterly report to augment the custodian statements. The quarterly report should contain supplemental information that is not included in the custodial statements such as investment allocation and performance.

When shopping for a financial advisor, find someone who is going to do a financial plan with you on a regular basis. Your advisor needs to get a clear picture of you, your spending, your savings, and your goals/objectives. Find an advisor who is using an investment policy statement so that they can determine your comfort level when it comes to risk and returns. I always find it difficult when a prospective client asks *"Can I just pay you for investment advice and nothing more."* I can't give investment advice in a vacuum.

It isn't fair to me and it isn't fair to the client. I need to have a plan for every investor prior to recommending an investment strategy or portfolio allocation. Personally, I would be very wary of anyone who agreed to simply review your portfolio for you without knowing who you are and where you are in terms of your overall financial picture.

When it comes to financial planning, unfortunately, anyone can call themselves a financial planner. There are, however, registration boards that have high standards and requirements that certify financial planners. Be sure to look for someone who has completed a certified financial planning program. A Certified Financial Planner (CFP®) undergoes an extensive training program. Furthermore, CFPs are held to the highest ethical and educational standards.

While hiring a financial planner may be costly, some advisors lower their subsequent fee to update a plan. The initial outlay involves a fair amount of data collection and analysis. This is an important step. You need someone who will take a complete inventory of your financial status. You need someone who will listen to you and who knows what is important to you. You need someone who will explain the investment process and who will be with you every step of the way. Again, after the financial plan is complete, you can sometimes update and maintain the plan at a lower cost.

DOES AN ANNUITY HAVE A PLACE
IN YOUR PORTFOLIO?

Elderly people are often encouraged to buy annuities. A colleague of mine went through her parents' portfolio when her mom and dad entered a nursing home. She discovered that her parents had somehow accumulated ten different annuities. Some agent was probably knocking at their door every month, selling them a new product. There are unethical brokers whose desire to make a quick profit by selling an insurance product overrides what is best for the customer. Unfortunately, this was the situation with my colleague's parents.

I do not mean to suggest that every annuity is bad. There are some very good annuities available on the market. If you can get an annuity with a fixed rate of return, you might not necessarily care that it comes with a high internal fee. If someone told me I would receive a 6 percent guaranteed return, and I knew I only needed 5 percent for my fixed income allocation, why should I be concerned about the internal fees? I am earning 1 percent more than what I need, and it is guaranteed—be somewhat cautious here, be sure you know how the investment works and if the return is net of fees. Make sure that you understand the product that you are buying, and if someone is not willing to explain it to you, walk away. Furthermore, this should not be your only investment. The annuity should be a complement to your other investment holdings.

Most importantly, if anyone tells you, "This deal is only available today," or tries to pressure you to buy immediately, that is a big red flag. You should not be pressured into doing anything. Don't walk, *run*. Chances are when most annuity products become available, there is not "a limited time only." It is going to be there tomorrow or next month or next year. The only thing that might change is the interest rate.

One last point about annuities: If you put money into what is called a single life immediate annuity, at your death that money is gone. If you have children or if you have a spouse, they are not getting a residual cash balance. The insurance company keeps the rest of your money. Don't sign off on something like that unless you discuss it with your spouse first. As mentioned earlier, you have payout options when it comes to immediate annuities.

Whatever you do, don't make any rash decisions. Feel comfortable with the person you are dealing with, and don't feel pressured by anyone to have to do something right then and there. Make sure that you know what you are getting. And if it sounds too good to be true, it probably is.

In Closing...

Life is unpredictable, but good organization, comprehensive preparation, and adequate education can lead to the implementation of a personalized plan that can prepare you for what may come your way. My intention for writing this book is to alleviate the financial stress that results from transitional events that occur in our lives. Understanding the process before, during and after a transitional phase in your life and navigating through it with the advice in this book will provide you with a sense of empowerment and peace.

I personally have experienced many hardships in my life that include divorce, death of a loved one, the unexpected loss of a job as well as an incurable illness. No one ever said life was easy, and it may appear that bad things only happen to you, but that is not true. Everyone will undergo life-changing events, and having at least your financial and legal affairs in place will help carry you through some of the most difficult times. My hope is that this book provides guidance for your more secure financial future and inspires you to take charge of your life and your well-being. I appreciate your feedback.

You are welcome to email me at info@womensfinancialhelp.com or visit my website: Womensfinancialhelp.com.

Appendix

Balance Sheet

Balance Sheet				
Assets	**John**	**Julie**	**Joint - ROS**	**Total**
Home	-	-	$ 825,000.00	$ 825,000.00
Cash Account	-	-	$ 5,000.00	$ 5,000.00
Every Day Checking	-	-	$ 7,622.00	$ 7,622.00
John & Julie's Joint Investment Acct	-	-	$ 219,000.00	$ 219,000.00
John's 401K	$ 312,000.00	-	-	$ 312,000.00
Julie's 403B	$ 120,000.00	-	-	$ 120,000.00
Julie's Roth IRA (converted)	-	$ 89,540.00	-	$ 89,540.00
Whole Life Policy on John	$ 50,000.00	-	-	$ 50,000.00
Jewelry	$ 2,500.00	$ 32,000.00	-	$ 34,500.00
Cars	-	-	$ 60,000.00	$ 60,000.00
Total Assets:	$ 484,500.00	$ 121,540.00	$ 1,116,622.00	$ 1,722,662.00
Liabilities	**John**	**Julie**	**Joint - ROS**	**Total**
Mortgage on Home	-	-	$ (426,385.00)	$ (426,385.00)
HELOC	-	-	$ (15,000.00)	$ (15,000.00)
Credit Cards	$ (3,200.00)	$ (245.00)	-	$ (3,445.00)
Total Liabilities:	$ (3,200.00)	$ (245.00)	$ (441,385.00)	$ (444,830.00)
Total Net Worth:	$ 487,700.00	$ 121,785.00	$ 1,558,007.00	$ 2,167,492.00

Budget/Cash Flow Sheet

Budget/Cash Flow Sheet

	Jan	Feb	Mar	Apr	May	Jun	Jul	Aug	Sep	Oct	Nov	Dec	Total
Opening balance	$1,200.00												
Income (after tax and benefits)													
Salary	$4,930.00	$4,930.00	$4,930.00	$4,930.00	$4,930.00	$4,930.00	$4,930.00	$4,930.00	$4,930.00	$4,930.00	$4,930.00	$4,930.00	$59,160.00
Interest/dividends	$50.00	$50.00	$50.00	$50.00	$50.00	$50.00	$50.00	$50.00	$50.00	$50.00	$50.00	$50.00	$600.00
Total Income	$4,980.00	$4,980.00	$4,980.00	$4,980.00	$4,980.00	$4,980.00	$4,980.00	$4,980.00	$4,980.00	$4,980.00	$4,980.00	$4,980.00	**$59,760.00**
Expenses													
Mortgage or rent	$1,500.00	$1,500.00	$1,500.00	$1,500.00	$1,500.00	$1,500.00	$1,500.00	$1,500.00	$1,500.00	$1,500.00	$1,500.00	$1,500.00	$18,000.00
Taxes	$500.00			$500.00				$500.00				$500.00	$2,000.00
Car payments	$295.00	$295.00	$295.00	$295.00	$295.00	$295.00	$295.00	$295.00	$295.00	$295.00	$295.00	$295.00	$3,540.00
Car maintenance													$0.00
Food	$390.00	$390.00	$390.00	$390.00	$390.00	$390.00	$390.00	$390.00	$390.00	$390.00	$390.00	$390.00	$4,680.00
Clothes misc shopping	$250.00	$250.00	$250.00	$250.00	$250.00	$250.00	$250.00	$250.00	$250.00	$250.00	$250.00	$250.00	$3,000.00
Cash withdrawals	$200.00	$200.00	$200.00	$200.00	$200.00	$200.00	$200.00	$200.00	$200.00	$200.00	$200.00	$200.00	$2,400.00
restaurants	$100.00	$100.00	$100.00	$100.00	$100.00	$100.00	$100.00	$100.00	$100.00	$100.00	$100.00	$100.00	$1,200.00
Kids expenses	$225.00	$225.00	$225.00	$225.00	$225.00	$225.00	$225.00	$225.00	$225.00	$225.00	$225.00	$225.00	$2,700.00
Professional fees				$850.00									$850.00
Pets	$50.00	$50.00	$50.00	$50.00	$50.00	$50.00	$50.00	$50.00	$50.00	$50.00	$50.00	$50.00	$600.00
phone/internet/cable	$180.00	$180.00	$180.00	$180.00	$180.00	$180.00	$180.00	$180.00	$180.00	$180.00	$180.00	$180.00	$2,160.00
Utilities (Electricity, Gas, Water)	$320.00	$320.00	$320.00	$120.00	$120.00	$120.00	$120.00	$120.00	$120.00	$120.00	$320.00	$320.00	$2,440.00
Medication/copays/ deductible	$500.00	$500.00	$500.00	$500.00	$500.00	$100.00	$100.00	$100.00	$100.00	$100.00	$100.00	$100.00	$3,200.00
Dental Expenses	$100.00	$100.00	$100.00	$100.00	$100.00	$100.00	$100.00	$100.00	$100.00	$100.00	$100.00	$100.00	$1,200.00
Home Insurance	$75.00	$75.00	$75.00	$75.00	$75.00	$75.00	$75.00	$75.00	$75.00	$75.00	$75.00	$75.00	$900.00
Loan payments	$125.00	$125.00	$125.00	$125.00	$125.00	$125.00	$125.00	$125.00	$125.00	$125.00	$125.00	$125.00	$1,500.00
Vacation/travel							$3,500.00						$3,500.00
Other expenses	$50.00	$50.00	$50.00	$50.00	$50.00	$50.00	$50.00	$50.00	$50.00	$50.00	$50.00	$50.00	$600.00
Total Expenses	$4,860.00	$4,360.00	$4,360.00	$5,510.00	$4,160.00	$3,760.00	$7,260.00	$4,260.00	$3,760.00	$3,760.00	$3,960.00	$4,460.00	**$ 54,470.00**
Net Monthly CashFlow	$120.00	$620.00	$620.00	-$530.00	$820.00	$1,220.00	-$2,280.00	$720.00	$1,220.00	$1,220.00	$1,020.00	$520.00	$5,290.00
Cumulative CashFlow	$120.00	$740.00	$1,360.00	$830.00	$1,650.00	$2,870.00	$590.00	$1,310.00	$2,530.00	$3,750.00	$4,770.00	$5,290.00	

HIPPAA Release Form *page 1 of 2*

Massachusetts Department of Public Health
Authorization for Release of Information
Permission to Share Information

If you want the _____ to share information about you with another person or
(Fill in name of person or organization)
organization, please make sure that you fill out all of the sections below (Sections I-VI). This will tell us what
information you want us to share and who to share it with. If you leave any sections blank, with the exception of
Section II (B), your permission will not be valid, and we will not be able to share your information with the person(s)
or organization you listed on this form.

SECTION I
I, _____, give my permission for _____
(print your name)   (Fill in name of person or
organization)
to share the information about me that I list in Section II with the person(s) or organization that I list in Section V.

SECTION II
A. Health and Personal Information
Please describe the information you want the _____ to share about you.
(Fill in name of person or organization)
Please include any dates and details you want to share.
_____
_____
_____
_____

**B. Permission about Specific Health Information. Only if you choose to share any of the following
information, please write your initials on the line:**
____I specifically give permission, as required by M.G.L. c. 111, § 70F, to share information in my record about HIV
antibody and antigen testing, and HIV/AIDS diagnosis or HIV/AIDS treatment.
____I specifically give permission, as required by M.G.L. c. 111, §70G, to share information in my record about my
genetic information.
____I specifically give permission to share information in my record about alcohol or drug treatment. If this
information is shared, I understand that a specific notice required by 42 CFR, Part 2 shall be included prohibiting the
redisclosure of this confidential information.

SECTION III – Reason for Sharing this Information
Please describe the reason(s) for sharing this information.   If you do not want to list reasons, you may simply write:
"at my request," if you are initiating the request.
_____
_____
_____

SECTION IV – Who May Share This Information
I give permission to the person or organization listed below to share the information I listed in Section II:

_____
Name
_____
Organization
_____
Address
_____

HIPPAA Release Form *page 2 of 2*

Massachusetts Department of Public Health
Authorization for Release of Information

SECTION V – Who May Receive My Information

The person or organization listed in Section IV may share the information I listed in Section II with this person(s) or organization:

_____
Name
_____
Organization
_____
Address

I understand that the person(s) or organization listed in this section may not be covered by federal or state privacy laws, and that they may be able to further share the information that is given to them.

SECTION VI – How Long This Permission Lasts

This permission to share my information is good until _____.
Indicate date or event
If I do not list a date or event, this permission will last for one year from the date it is signed.

- I understand that I can change my mind and cancel this permission at any time. To do this, I need to write a letter to _____, and send it or bring it to the place where I am now giving
(Fill in name of person or organization)
this permission (or fill in specific location) If the information has already been given out by, I understand that it is too late for me to change my mind and cancel the permission.

- I understand that I do not have to give permission to share my information with the person(s) or organization I listed in Section V.

- I understand that if I choose not to give this permission or if I cancel my permission, I will still be able to receive any treatment or benefits that I am entitled to, as long as this information is not needed to determine if I am eligible for services or to pay for the services that I receive.

SECTION V – Signature
Please sign and date this form, and print your name.

_____   _____
Your Signature   Date

_____
Print Your Name

If this form is being filled out by someone who has the legal authority to act for you (such as the parent of a minor child, a court appointed guardian or executor, a custodial parent, or a health care agent), please:

Print the name of the person filling out this form: _____

Signature of the person filling out this form: _____

Describe how this person has legal authority for this individual: _____

Massachusetts Affidavit of Domicile

AFFIDAVIT OF DOMICILE	Docket No.	Commonwealth of Massachusetts The Trial Court Probate and Family Court

Estate of: ▼ **Division**

First Name   Middle Name   Last Name

Date of Death:

I, _____ the _____
    First Name   M.I.   Last Name   relationship

of the decedent do hereby state from my personal knowledge that the decedent was domiciled at:

_____ , Massachusetts
(Address)   (Apt, Unit, No. etc.)   (City/Town)   (County)

at the time of death based on the following facts.

☐ The decedent, at the time of death, was a record owner of the property;

☐ The decedent's spouse continues to reside at the property;

☐ Many of the decedent's personal effects are located at the property;

☐ The decedent filed his/her last income tax return for the year _____ indicating that his/her residence was at the address.

☐ The decedent at the time of his/her death was living at the above address and had lived there since _____
    (year)

☐ The decedent's residence at:

_____
(Address)   (Apt, Unit, No. etc.)   (City/Town)   (State)   (Zip)

was of a temporary nature due to:

and at no time did the decedent intend to abandon his/her domicile at:

_____ , Massachusetts
(City/Town)   (County)

☐ Other:

SIGNED UNDER THE PENALTIES OF PERJURY

I certify under the penalties of perjury that the foregoing statements are true to the best of my knowledge and belief.

Date _____

_____
Signature

_____
Print Name

_____
(Address)   (Apt, Unit, No. etc.)

_____
(City/Town)   (State)   (Zip)

Primary Phone #:

Reset Form

Massachusetts Health Care Proxy *page 1 of 4*

NOTICE: The following form is protected by federal copyright law. An individual may download and print a single copy for his or her personal use. Health care organizations, clinicians, professionals, and others can purchase the form in quantity, or secure a license from Massachusetts Health Decisions, the nonprofit publisher of the form and educational materials related to the Massachusetts Health Care Proxy. The form is available in English, Braille, and many non-English languages. Contact MHD at: <proxy@masshealthdecisions.org> For $6 postpaid, individuals may order a complete information packet including two copies of the form, a basic brochure called "Making Choices...", and a 16-page "User's Guide" in question-and-answer format. Massachusetts Health Decisions, Publications, PO Box 1407, Apex, NC 27502.

MASSACHUSETTS HEALTH CARE PROXY
Information, Instructions, and Form

What does the Health Care Proxy Law allow?

The **Health Care Proxy** is a simple legal document that allows you to name someone you know and trust to make health care decisions for you if, for any reason and at any time, you become unable to make or communicate those decisions. It is an important document, however, because it concerns not only the choices you make about your health care, but also the relationships you have with your physician, family, and others who may be involved with your care. Read this and follow the instructions to ensure that your wishes are honored.

Under the Health Care Proxy Law (Massachusetts General Laws, Chapter 201D), any competent adult 18 years of age or over may use this form to appoint a Health Care Agent. You (known as the "Principal") can appoint any adult EXCEPT the administrator, operator, or employee of a health care facility such as a hospital or nursing home where you are a patient or resident UNLESS that person is also related to you by blood, marriage, or adoption. Whether or not you live in Massachusetts, you can use this form if you receive your health care in Massachusetts.

What can my Agent do?

Your Agent will make decisions about your health care *only* when you are, for some reason, unable to do that yourself. This means that your Agent can act for you if you are temporarily unconscious, in a coma, or have some other condition in which you cannot make or communicate health care decisions. Your Agent cannot act for you until your doctor determines, in writing, that you lack the ability to make health care decisions. Your doctor will tell you of this if there is any sign that you would understand it.

Acting with your authority, your Agent can make any health care decision that you could, if you were able. If you give your Agent full authority to act for you, he or she can consent to or refuse any medical treatment, including treatment that could keep you alive.

Your Agent will make decisions for you only after talking with your doctor or health care provider, and after fully considering all the options regarding diagnosis, prognosis, and treatment of your illness or condition. Your Agent has the legal right to get any information, including confidential medical information, necessary to make informed decisions for you.

Your Agent will make health care decisions for you according to your wishes or according to his/her assessment of your wishes, including your religious or moral beliefs. You may wish to talk first with your doctor, religious advisor, or other people before giving instructions to your Agent. It is very important that you talk with your Agent so that he or she knows what is important to you. If your Agent does not know what your wishes would be in a particular situation, your Agent will decide based on what he or she thinks would be in your best interests. After your doctor has determined that you lack the ability to make health care decisions, if you still object to any decision made by your Agent, your own decisions will be honored unless a Court determines that you lack capacity to make health care decisions.

Massachusetts Health Care Proxy *page 2 of 4*

Your Agent's decisions will have the same authority as yours would, if you were able, and will be honored over those of any other person, except for any limitation you yourself made, or except for a Court Order specifically overriding the Proxy.

How do I fill out the form?

1. At the top of the form, print your full name and address. Print the name, address, and phone number of the person you choose as your Health Care Agent. (**Optional:** If you think your Agent might not be available at any future time, you may name a second person as an Alternate Agent. Your Alternate Agent will be called if your Agent is unwilling or unable to serve.)

2. Setting limits on your Agent's authority might make it difficult for your Agent to act for you in an unexpected situation. If you want your Agent to have full authority to act for you, leave the limitations space blank. However, if you want to limit the kinds of decisions you would want your Agent or Alternate Agent to make for you, include them in the blank.

3. **BEFORE** you sign, be sure you have two adults present who will be witnesses and watch you sign the document. The only people who cannot serve as witnesses are your Agent and Alternate Agent. Then sign and date the document yourself. (Or, if you are physically unable, have someone other than either witness sign your name at your direction. The person who signs your name for you should put his/her own name and address in the spaces provided.)

4. Have your witnesses fill in the date, sign their names and print their names and addresses.

5. **OPTIONAL:** On the back of the form are statements to be signed by your Agent and any Alternate Agent. This is not required by law, but is recommended to ensure that you have talked with the person or persons who may have to make important decisions about your care and that each of them realizes the importance of the task they may have to do.

Who should have the original and copies?

After you have filled in the form, remove this information page and make at least four photocopies of the form. Keep the original yourself where it can be found easily (*not* in your safe deposit box). Give copies to your doctor and/or health plan to put into your medical record. Give copies to your Agent and any Alternate Agent. You can give additional copies to family members, your clergy and/or lawyer, and other people who may be involved in your health care decisionmaking.

How can I revoke or cancel the document?

Your Health Care Proxy is revoked when any of the following four things happens:

1. You sign another Health Care Proxy later on.
2. You legally separate from or divorce your spouse who is named in the Proxy as your Agent.
3. You notify your Agent, your doctor, or other health care provider, orally or in writing, that you want to revoke your Health Care Proxy.
4. You do anything else that clearly shows you want to revoke the Proxy, for example, tearing up or destroying the Proxy, crossing it out, telling other people, etc.

AFTER FILLING IN THE FORM, REMOVE THIS INSTRUCTION PAGE. BE SURE TO TALK WITH YOUR AGENT.

Massachusetts Health Care Proxy *page 3 of 4*

YOUR BIRTH DATE (m/d/y)
____/____/____

MASSACHUSETTS HEALTH CARE PROXY

1 I, _____, residing at
(Principal: PRINT your name)

_____
(Street)   (City/town)   (State/ZIP)

appoint as my **Health Care Agent**: _____
(Name of person you choose as Agent)

of_____
(Street)   (City/town)   (State/ZIP)

Agent's tel (h) _____ (w) _____ E-mail _____

OPTIONAL: If my agent is unwilling or unable to serve, then I appoint as my **Alternate Agent**:

_____
(Name of person you choose as Alternate Agent)

of_____
(Street)   (City/town)   (State/ZIP)   (Phone)

2 My Agent shall have the authority to make all health care decisions for me, including decisions about life-sustaining treatment, subject to any limitations I state below, if I am unable to make health care decisions myself. My Agent's authority becomes effective if my attending physician determines in writing that I lack the capacity to make or to communicate health care decisions. My Agent is then to have the same authority to make health care decisions as I would if I had the capacity to make them **EXCEPT** (here list the limitations, *if any*, you wish to place on your Agent's authority):

I direct my Agent to make health care decisions based on my Agent's assessment of my personal wishes. If my personal wishes are unknown, my Agent is to make health care decisions based on my Agent's assessment of my best interests. Photocopies of this Health Care Proxy shall have the same force and effect as the original and may be given to other health care providers.

3   **Signed**:_____ **Date:** ___/___/___ (mo/day/yr)

Complete only if Principal is physically unable to sign: I have signed the Principal's name above at his/her direction in the presence of the Principal and two witnesses.

_____   _____
(Name)   (Street)

                                         _____
                                         (City/town)   (State/ZIP)

4 **WITNESS STATEMENT:** We, the undersigned, each witnessed the signing of this Health Care Proxy by the Principal or at the direction of the Principal and state that the Principal appears to be at least 18 years of age, of sound mind and under no constraint or undue influence. Neither of us is named as the Health Care Agent or Alternate Agent in this document.
In our presence, on this day 08 /08 / 16 (mo / day / yr).

Witness #1 _____   Witness #2 _____
           (Signature)   (Signature)

Name (print) _____   Name (print) _____

Address _____   Address _____

_____   _____

Massachusetts Health Care Proxy *page 4 of 4*

| 5 | **Statements of Health Care Agent and Alternate Agent (OPTIONAL)** |

Health Care Agent: I have been named by the Principal as the Principal's **Health Care Agent** by this Health Care Proxy. I have read this document carefully, and have personally discussed with the Principal his/her health care wishes at a time of possible incapacity. I know the Principal and accept this appointment freely. I am not an operator, administrator or employee of a hospital, clinic, nursing home, rest home, Soldiers Home or other health facility where the Principal is presently a patient or resident or has applied for admission. But if I am a person so described, I am also related to the Principal by blood, marriage, or adoption. If called upon and to the best of my ability, I will try to carry out the Principal's wishes.

(Signature of **Health Care Agent**)_____

Alternate Agent: I have been named by the Principal as the Principal's **Alternate Agent** by this Health Care Proxy. I have read this document carefully, and have personally discussed with the Principal his/her health care wishes at a time of possible incapacity. I know the Principal and accept this appointment freely. I am not an operator, administrator or employee of a hospital, clinic, nursing home, rest home, Soldiers Home or other health facility where the Principal is presently a patient or resident or has applied for admission. But if I am a person so described, I am also related to the Principal by blood, marriage, or adoption. If called upon and to the best of my ability, I will try to carry out the Principal's wishes.

(Signature of **Alternate Agent**)_____

*   *   *   *   *

**Health Care Proxy developed by Massachusetts Health Decisions in association with
the following member organizations of the Massachusetts Health Care Proxy Task Force:**

Boston University Schools of Medicine and Public Health:
  Law, Medicine, and Ethics Program
Deaconess ElderCare Program
Hospice Federation of Massachusetts
Massachusetts Bar Association
Massachusetts Department of Public Health
Massachusetts Executive Office of Elder Affairs
Massachusetts Federation of Nursing Homes
Massachusetts Health Decisions

Massachusetts Hospital Association
Massachusetts Medical Society
Massachusetts Nurses Association
Medical Center of Central Massachusetts
Suffolk University Law School:
  Elder Law Clinic
University of Massachusetts at Boston:
  The Gerontology Institute
Visiting Nurse Associations of Massachusetts

For prices and information on quantity orders, or for non-English language licensing, please contact non-profit
Massachusetts Health Decisions
Email: proxy@masshealthdecisions.org

rev. 1/15

Parental Nomination of Guardian *page 1 of 2*

PARENTAL NOMINATION OF GUARDIAN

I, _____(name), resident of and domiciled at

_____(address)

_____(city),

_____(county), Massachusetts,

_____(zip code) make, publish and declare this Parental Appointment of Guardian, revoking all prior appointments at any time heretofore made by me.

Listed below are my children and their dates of birth:

Child(ren) Name(s):	Date of Birth:

Should any child(ren) of mine be under the age of 18 as of the date of my death, I appoint:

_____ (name of person to be appointed guardian) as

his/her/their legal guardian.

No Guardian shall be required to file or furnish any bond, surety or other security in any jurisdiction.

IN WITNESS WHEREOF, I, _____(name of parent(s)), sign my

name to this instrument as a Parental Nomination of Guardian this _____ day of _____, 20___, and

being first duly sworn, do hereby declare to the undersigned authority that I sign and execute this

instrument, that I sign it willingly, that I execute it as my free and voluntary act and deed for the purposes

therein expressed, and that I am at least eighteen years of age, of sound mind, and under no constraint,

duress, fraud or undue influence. I also have affixed my initials on the bottom of each of the preceding

pages hereof.

_____   _____
Name of parent   Name of parent

We,_____

_____, the witnesses, sign our names to this instrument, and, being first duly sworn, do each hereby

Parental Nomination of Guardian *page 2 of 2*

declare to the undersigned authority that _____(name of parent(s)), signed and executed this Parental Nomination of Guardian and that she signed it willingly, and that each of us, in the presence and hearing of the Signor, and each other, hereby signs this Parental Nomination of Guardian as witness to the Parent's signing, and that that to the best of each of our knowledge the Testatrix is at least eighteen years of age, of sound mind, and under no constraint , duress, fraud or undue influence.

_____   _____
Witness   Witness
Address: Address:

_____   _____

_____   _____

COMMONWEALTH OF MASSACHUSETTS

_____ ss.

_____

Subscribed, sworn to and acknowledged before me by the said _____

(name of parent), and subscribed and sworn to before me by the said

_____, as witnesses, this _____ day

of _____, 20__.

_____
Notary Public
My Commission expires on:

It would also be a good idea to have a will prepared to deal with who should be appointed financial guardian for the child.

Printed in the USA
CPSIA information can be obtained
at www.ICGtesting.com
JSHW012036140824
68134JS00033B/3081